Grammar Grams II

Stephen K. Tollefson
University of California, Berkeley

HarperCollins*Publishers*

This book is for all my family,
and especially for Sally:
"Never again would birds' song
be the same.
And to do that to birds was why
she came."—Robert Frost

Sponsoring Editor: Jane Kinney

Project Editior: Thomas R. Farrell

Design Supervisor: Dorothy Bungert

Production Administrator: Paula Keller

Cover Design: Edward Smith Design

Compositor: Publishing Synthesis, Ltd.

Printer and Binder: Courier Kendallville, Inc.

Cover Printer: New England Book Components, Inc.

GRAMMAR GRAMS II

Library of Congress Cataloging-in-Publication Data
(Revised for vol. 2)

Tollefson, Stephen K.
Grammar grams.

Cover title.
Vol. 2 published by HarperCollins.
1. English language—Grammar—1950- . 2. English Language—Rhetoric. I. Title.
PE1112.Y65 1989
425 88-25183
ISBN 0-06-046687-1 (v.1)
ISBN 0-06-046738-X (v.2)

91 92 93 94 9 8 7 6 5 4 3 2 1

CONTENTS

INTRODUCTION 4

VOLUME I
Hors d'Oeuvres

No. 1 The War Between the North and the South 5
The two vocabularies in English

No. 2 You Blocks, You Stones, You Worse Than Senseless Things 6
Who died and made you a critic?

No. 3 Grammar Grams: The Test 7

VOLUME II
Verbs and Friends

No. 1 Particle Physics 8
The science of two-word verbs

No. 2 Duck! Quick(ly)! 9

No. 3 Play It, Sam, Again 10
Where adverbs and adjectives go if they don't go to Casablanca

No. 4 I Think; Therefore, I Feel 11
Some words with no backbone

No. 5 A Little Present from the Grammar Gram 12

VOLUME III:
Rebel Without a Clause

No. 1 Why Did You Hit Your Little Sister? 13
Just because

No. 2 Because of the Wonderful Things He Does 14
The Wizard of Oz and bad grammar

No. 3 Subordination and Humiliation 15
Use one to prevent the other.

No. 4 Conjunction Dysfunction 16
And, but, or, nor, for, so, yet

No. 5 If at First You Don't Succeed . . . 17
Revising is reseeing.

VOLUME IV
Questions

No. 1 Jeopardy! 18
Please don't phrase your answer in the form of a question.

No. 2 Is This a Good Grammar Gram, or What? 19
Rhetorical questions

No. 3 The Camelopard Sentence 20
Sentences that are half statement and half question

VOLUME V
Beginnings and Endings (and a Middle)

No. 1 Let's Get This Baby off the Ground 21
Six rules to help you get going

No. 2 In the Beginning Was the Word 22
"Ninety-nine percent of pieces of writing fail in the first three sentences."—A famous grammar guru

No. 3 May I Take Your Order, Please? 23
Please read this Grammar Gram by following the numbers.

No. 4 Repent, for the End Is Near 24
How to begin to conclude a piece of writing

No. 5 Famous Last Words 25
How to conclude a piece of writing

VOLUME VI
The Big Picture

No. 1 The Theory of Relativity 26

No. 2 The Space-Time Continuum 27
If it's so unimportant, why did you spend three paragraphs on it?

No. 3 Concession Stands 28
Git yer hot dogs, sodas, opposing arguments.

No. 4 Being Driven to Abstraction 29
On a concrete highway

No. 5 Evidence 30
How do we know that the can contains spinach, Mr. Popeye?

VOLUME VII
Yours, Mine, and Ours

No. 1 Two, Four, Six, Eight, What Do We Appreciate? 31
I appreciate your calling; I don't appreciate you whining, however.

No. 2 This Yam Is Your Yam, This Yam Is My Yam 32
Problems with possessives and a tribute to Yma Sumac

No. 3 Me, Myself, and I 33
May the grammar doctor check your reflexives?

No. 4 The Man with Two Brains 34
A good Steve Martin movie and a problem with singulars and plurals

No. 5 Us, the People 35
Let's not make a federal case out of this.

VOLUME VIII
Choices

No. 1 That's All Very *Well* and *Good* 36
But what's the difference?

No. 2 The Sun Also Rises, Too 37
When and where to use *also, too,* and *in addition*

No. 3 Evo or Devo? 38
Changes in the meanings and uses of words

No. 4 Can You Be More Specific? 39

VOLUME IX
This, That, and the Other Thing

No. 1 Double Indemnity 40
Making the reader pay twice for the same idea

No. 2 May We Check Your References? 41
This, that, these, those, they, them, it

No. 3 Can't We Agree on Anything? 42

No. 4 Take *That,* and *That,* and *That* 43
Three times to use *that* word

No. 5 The *Today* Show 44
With uninvited guest, the possessive apostrophe

VOLUME X
Fun, Fun, Fun

No. 1 The Periodic Table 45
We're withholding information.

No. 2 Serious and Cumulative 46
Are those sentences or clouds?

No. 3 Eleven Fun Things You Can Do in Writing 47

No. 4 The Ski Punks Versus The Ten Commandments 48
Repetition for emphasis

No. 5 The Meek Shall Inherit the Earth 49
The power of small words

VOLUME XI
Around the World

No. 1 Fora and Fauna, or Here's Symposia for You 50
Plurals of foreign words

No. 2 *Sic Transit Gloria Mundi* 51
Fun Foreign Frases

No. 3 Abbrev. 52
Common abbreviations of foreign words

No. 4 It's Not Easy Being Green 53

VOLUME XII
Punctuation

No. 1 Grammar and the Single Comma 54

No. 2 Comma, Comma, Down, Doobie, Do, Down, Down 55
The first degree of parenthetical ideas

No. 3 And Death, I Think, Is No Parenthesis 56
The second degree of parenthetical ideas

No. 4 The 100-Yard Dash: Punctuation for the Lazy? 57
Give 'em the third degree of parenthetical ideas.

No. 5 What's All That Bracket About? 58
You're [*sic*], [*sic*], [*sic*].

No. 6 Hyphen-nation 59

No. 7 Spacing: The Final Frontier 60
Rules for confronting space

VOLUME XIII
Games, Tests, and Trivia

No. 1 A Hunting We Will Go 61
Impractical language information: terms of venery

No. 2 The Berkeley Test of Basic Religious and Gramattical Concepts 62

No. 3 Manners in Language 63
Thank you for not expressing your true feelings.

No. 4 The Root's the Same 64
An etymology game

Index 65

Introduction

Dear Grammar Gram:

In the first *Grammar Grams*, you implied—I am quite sure—that you said everything you had to say about grammar and writing. Now here's a second volume, with even more. What do you have to say for yourself?

Signed,

Disgusted

Dear Disgusted:

The Grammar Gram never implied any such thing; you only incorrectly inferred it (see *Grammar Grams II*, Vol. VIII, No.3, on *implied* and *inferred*). You should also check Vol. XII, No. 4, to see if those dashes you used are correct. And while you're at it, you might find Vol. XII, No. 7, revealing. It will show you how to space between the closing of a letter and your signature. You see, then, that we still have a great deal to do; let's get going.

The first book of *Grammar Grams* grew out of a newsletter for staff at the University of California at Berkeley. Its purpose was to provide quick, clear responses to the kinds of questions all writers face as they write; this second book follows the same principles. The books consists of short, almost telegraphic explanations and discussions covering not only grammar, sentence structure, and style but also questions of format, vocabulary use, and editing.

This second book continues where the first book left off. Just as the first book discussed semi-colons and colons, for instance, this book adds discussions of dashes and parentheses. The first book discussed modification and parallel structure; this book adds agreement and reference to the discussion.

But this book is not merely more of the same. While continuing to adhere to the one-subject-per-page rule, in some cases it digs a little deeper than the first book. The first book devoted one Grammar Gram to all the general rules for commas. In the current book, one Grammmar Gram is devoted to describing when to use single commas and another to when to use commas in pairs. In the first book, one Grammar Gram discussed the differences among *because*, *since*, and *so*; here, two Grammar Grams deal with uses of *because*.

In addition, this book introduces some new and important areas for discussion. There are Grammar Grams on how to begin and conclude pieces of writing and an important series (Vol. VI) on some larger issues in writing, including the use of evidence, the relative size of paragraphs, and levels of abstraction. The ways in which Grammar Grams approach some of these topics is different from those seen in most standard books on writing. In the volume titled "Fun, Fun, Fun," (Vol. X), readers learn how to construct cumulative and periodic sentences, how to use repetition for emphasis, and how to do "Eleven Fun Things" in writing.

Readers will note that the word *essay* does not occur very often in this book; in its place is the somewhat more cumbersome *piece of writing* or an equivalent. Unless specifically noted (how to space business letters), everything in this book applies to essays, but it applies to most other writing, too—business reports, term papers, letters, memos. The aim of not using *essay*, then, is to be inclusive rather than exclusive. Since secretaries, lawyers, and other business people use this book, there is no reason that students shouldn't use it for work beyond their writing courses.

Some aspects of this new book are in direct response to requests. This book contains an index because teachers asked for one. A number of the current Grammar Grams have been developed because someone said, "You really should do one on that subject." For example, Vol. XI, No. 4 ("It's Not Easy Being Green") deals with an issue that currently confuses many people: how to refer to ethnic and racial groups.

The general principles remain the same in this second book as in the first. Because language changes, our rules are merely guides, and the Grammar Grams try to point out where changes are occurring. The discussions must be short, so they are necessarily selective. And the tone is friendly and conversational.

This book concludes with several Grammar Grams that are quizzes, games, and trivia (with a point) about language. This, too, seems a natural outgrowth of the original idea of Grammar Grams, which is to learn about language but to have a little fun while learning.

Stephen K. Tollefson

THE WAR BETWEEN THE NORTH AND THE SOUTH

The two vocabularies in English

Would you rather communicate with your supervisor or talk to your boss? Would you rather read a dirty Grammar Gram or an obscene one?

In English, we are lucky to have what amounts to parallel vocabularies: one from southern Europe (Latin and Greek roots) and the other from northern Europe (German, Anglo-Saxon, and Scandinavian roots). For instance, *communicate* and *supervisor* are from Latin, while *talk* and *boss* are from, respectively, Anglo-Saxon and Old High German (an old form of German, not an old German smoking marijuana). Likewise, *dirty* is from the north and *obscene* is from the south.

We sometimes use the words from the two vocabularies interchangeably because they are similar in meaning. Usually, we don't run into trouble choosing one or the other. However, the pairs of words are not identical: for instance, *communicate* covers a wider range of activities than *talk* does, so we can't always say "talk" when we mean "communicate."

Here's a list that just scratches the surface of the parallel vocabularies:

SOUTH	NORTH
firmament	sky
perspire	sweat
intellect	mind, brain
perish	die
pyrotechnics	fireworks
labor	work
attorney	lawyer
automobile	car

Some patterns emerge from looking at this list. We see that first, the words from the north are usually shorter. Second, the northern words often have a harsher sound with harder consonants. And finally, the southern words are ones that we tend to consider more intellectual and refined. Of course, that's simply not true. But if you listen to people who you think are trying to sound intellectual, they will almost always aim for the southern words. But people who are truly *smart* (northern) or *intellectual* (southern) will use a combination of both vocabularies, choosing the right word for the situation.

Based on the patterns just described, try to identify the origin of the following words. If you aren't sure, check the dictionary.

auditorium	theater	walk	ambulate	think	contemplate
flying	aviation	to exist	to be	amphibian	toad
tolerate	put up with	admire	look up to		

Remember, neither vocabulary is better than the other. The south may have given us *rhinitis*, a word favored by doctors to mean "runny nose," but the north gave us *snout, snort, sneeze,* and *snot*, for which we should be eternally grateful.

YOU BLOCKS, YOU STONES, YOU WORSE THAN SENSELESS THINGS

Who died and made you a critic?

At some point, we are all called upon to offer our opinion of someone else's writing: a classmate's essay, a colleague's paper, or a secretary's memo. Here are some simple rules and reminders.

1. Criticize only when asked to do so.
The Grammar Gram is often tempted to point out an error in a letter, a sign, or an article. This would not be a good thing to do. Exceptions: If you're the boss, you get to do whatever you want to. Besides, grammar errors by those who work for you reflect badly on you. Sometimes in the writing of a colleague, classmate, or friend, you might also point out an error that might embarrass that person, but only after you've read the rest of this page.

2. Abide by the golden rule.
Do unto others as you would have them do unto you. When pointing out problems or errors in someone's writing, be kind. But don't turn into a spineless head-nodder. "My, that's nice" can actually be offensive.

3. Use the Alice Roosevelt Longworth antirule.
She said, "If you can't say anything nice about someone, come sit here beside me." This doesn't work when talking about writing. Always start with a positive comment or two about the writing, even if you have to play fast and loose with reality. And be specific about what is good.

4. Beware the bold pronouncement.
Never, ever, never, no, do not ever make statements such as "This sentence is wrong." Fifty percent of the time, you will be wrong yourself when you say that. Even if you're right, you'll probably lose a good working relationship or a friendship. (See Rule 2 above.) The bold pronouncement also makes your motives as a critic suspect; it will sound like your goal is not to improve the writing but simply to point out errors.

5. Violate two of the Grammar Gram's rules.

In writing, we should try to avoid starting sentences with phrases such as "I think that ...," and we should avoid being overly tentative by using such words as *might* and *perhaps.* These are the very things we do use, however, when talking about someone's writing: "I think that sentence might look better if it began with a capital letter."

6. Don't simply point out errors; suggest alternatives.
Don't say, "Your last sentence stinks, you know," but say, "Let's try wording that last sentence this way."

7. Explain yourself.
Unless the reason for a change is obvious (a spelling error, for example), explain the change as best you can: "Let's change *it* here to *they,* because the word should refer to masters of the universe, which is plural."

8. Ask questions.
Say, "What did you mean by this?" By asking questions, you can involve the writer: "What thought do you want to leave the reader with?" A question like this one makes the process of criticizing a collaboration.

By the way, the title of this Grammar Gram comes from Shakespeare's *Julius Caesar.* It's not what you get to yell at writers who ask for help.

GRAMMAR GRAMS: THE TEST

The letter below contains some of the ideas you will find discussed in *Grammar Grams II.* Use this test to determine where your strengths and weaknesses are and to learn to be your own best editor by finding and correcting problems. Suggested corrections appear in the second version of the letter, with references to the relevant Grammar Gram. By the way, not all the references are to problems; one or two may just point out interesting aspects of English.

To all employees:

Because of recent financial setbacks, we must begin layoffs immediately. The situation in our company is quite unique: we have no product to speak of, so we have no income. Discussions between the board of directors and myself have produced few results, except to set an agendum for our next meeting.

People often ask me will the company continue? And I reply, "A gaggle of geese couldn't keep this company down. The employees have done good, and I want to reward them. I don't want to aggravate the people who have kept this business afloat." I don't want to be known as a non-responsive boss (or should I say supervisor?).

I feel that all of you should use your brain and collectively develop some new approaches to our marketing problems. Too, you might consider giving up just a bit of your salary for the good of the company. That's what we need in this company.

Sincerely—
Cathy Ortega

The numbers in brackets indicate the volume and number of the relevant Grammar Gram.

To all employees:

Because we have suffered [III.2] recent financial setbacks, we must begin layoffs immediately. The situation in our company is unique [IX.1]: we have no income because [III.4] we have no product to speak of. Discussions between the board of directors and me [VII.3] have produced few results, except to set an agenda [XI.1] for our next meeting.

People often ask me if the company will continue [IV.1]. And I reply, "A gaggle of geese [XIII.1] couldn't keep this company down. The employees have done well [III.4], and I want to reward them. I don't want to irritate [VIII.3] the people who have kept this business afloat." I don't want to be known as a nonresponsive [XII.6] boss (or should I say supervisor [I.1]?).

I think [II.4] that all of you should use your brains [VIII.4] and collectively develop some new approaches to our marketing problems. In addition [VIII.2], you might consider giving up just a bit of your salary for the good of the company. We need more sacrifices like these [IX.2] in this company.

Sincerely, [XII.1]
Cathy Ortega [XII.7]

PARTICLE PHYSICS

The science of two-word verbs

You know that the Grammar Gram doesn't like to introduce specialized terminology unless it's absolutely essential. The following is not absolutely essential knowledge. But it's helpful and interesting. Honest. Like particles in physics (you know, quarks and things like that), adverbial particles (you don't need to remember the term, just the idea) in grammar are just little things: words that, by attaching themselves to verbs, change the meaning of those verbs. It's helpful to know about these words only because sometimes people confuse them with prepositions: *into* is a preposition, but *into* is also an adverbial particle. In case this is slightly confusing to you, let's rip some sentences apart; we'll underline the verbs:

Ginger ran into the hut.

Into the hut is here a prepositional phrase acting like an adverb. It tells us where Ginger ran: through the opening and inside the hut. Let's try it a different way:

Gilligan ran into the hut.

The verb is now *ran into*, and *the hut* is the object of the verb. Gilligan didn't go inside the hut; he crashed into it. How can we tell the difference between the two sentences? Obviously, Ginger wouldn't crash into the hut, but Gilligan would. (That is, we can usually tell from the context.) Here's another pair:

The Professor threw the coconut up in the air.

Up in the air is a prepositional phrase acting as an adverb telling us where the professor threw the coconut. But look at this:

Gilligan threw up the coconut.

The verb is *to throw up.* Gilligan ate too much and was sick. Now let's look at some verbs that have several different versions, including more than just one particle attached. The Grammar Gram won't comment on the meanings; you'll have to figure them out:

Mary Ann put the Skipper in a cast.
Mrs. Howell put up the money for the ocean view property.
Thurston won't put up with such shabby quarters.

In the middle sentence, we can see why the verb is *put up.* If it weren't, *up the money* would have to be a prepositional phrase like *up a tree.* And our response to it should be "Huh?" Finally, let's look at a common series of multiple-word verbs and their various meanings:

Did they agree to a three-hour tour? (Did they consent to it?)
Will they agree on a new name for the *Minnow*? (Will they reach an accord?)
They agreed with the natives that the island was too small. (They all had the same opinion.)
The Skipper and the Professor agreed about the need for a rescue. (They probably discussed it and reached a consensus.)

Next time, then, when you are chartering a boat, agree with the owner on the price before you agree to a tour unless you agree about how long it will last.

DUCK! QUICK(LY)!

Dear Grammar Gram:

Please settle a bet. Every week I play strip poker with some old friends. I *play well*, but some say I *play* much too *quickly*, while others claim I *play* just a little too *fast*. Here's the deal (ha! poker, get it?): I say you can always tell an adverb by its *ly* and my poker partners say I'm just really unruly. If I'm right, I'll donate my winnings to your favorite charity.

Signed,
Unruly and Proud

Dear Unruly:

Even bribes cannot change grammar; if they could, the Grammar Gram would be writing this from the beach in Hawaii. In writing, we need to know whether a word is an adjective or an adverb. Although the old *ly* guideline is OK as a general rule, not all adverbs end in *ly* and not all words ending in *ly* are adverbs:

The employees in this casino are a sickly group, aren't they?
This roulette wheel is unsightly.
Your unruly behavior is unbecoming.
The dealer looks silly in that suit of armor.
I don't see how I can play well today.
You deal too fast.

Oops. The Grammar Gram forgot to tell you which are adjectives and which are adverbs: *sickly, unsightly, silly,* and *unruly* are adjectives; *well* and *fast* are adverbs. The old *ly* rule doesn't always apply.

Some words can be either adjective or adverb:

Are you really a roulette dealer? (adjective)   You dealt those cards really fast. (adverb)

Note, however, that in these cases, especially the second one, *really* is better saved for spoken English. In written English, we would probably say, "You dealt those cards very fast." And in the first one we might say, "Are you actually a roulette dealer?"

Note: In some American dialects (and only in spoken language), we hear the following: "I'm feeling poorly" (adjective meaning "not well"). Be careful; this phrase works among the speakers of the dialect, but elsewhere it can sound like a Beverly Hillbilly-ism. We can say, however, "I'm feeling ill" (adjective meaning "not well") or "I'm feeling poor" (adjective meaning "lacking money").

Why do we care about whether a word is an adjective or an adverb? Because sometimes people try to say things like "She acted unruly today" or "He dresses unsightly" because they think that these words are adverbs. But they're adjectives and should be used in sentences such as "That unruly child of yours should be punished" and "My, that's an unsightly tie you have on."

Now for a moment, think of a sign on your neighborhood street. Should it say, "Drive slow; children present," or "Drive slowly; children present"? Did you finish this Grammar Gram quick, or did you finish it quickly?

Aloha,
The Grammar Gram

PLAY IT, SAM, AGAIN

Where adverbs and adjectives go if they don't go to Casablanca

On the set of the movie *Casablanca*, Humphrey Bogart probably didn't have a fit of bewilderment just before saying,

We'll always have Paris.

He certainly didn't mutter, "Where does that darn adverb go?" Most adverbs and adjectives seem to know their place—which is before the word they modify:

Ingrid suddenly developed a craving for Italian food. (adverb)
Casablanca means "white house" in Spanish. (adjective)

In languages such as Spanish, modifiers frequently come after the word they modify (*casa blanca* translates as "house white"), and occasionally they come after it in English too:

She looked longingly at the plate of pasta.

Although some people might think that Bogie violated a rule by sticking his adverb between the helping verb (*will*) and the main verb (*have*), it's nothing to lose sleep over. Some words, such as *only*, can be either adjectives or adverbs, depending on where we place them in a sentence, and we can change the meaning of a sentence just by moving a single word. It is important, then, to learn a little about where these words go. Notice how meaning changes in the following sentences. The word modified by *only* is underlined.

Only Louie allows gambling at Rick's place. (adjective; Louie is the only person who allows it; it's out of Rick's control.)
Louie only allows gambling at Ricks's place. (adverb; He allows it, but he doesn't condone it.)
Louie allows only gambling at Rick's place. (adjective; He doesn't allow any other activities.)
Louie allows gambling at Rick's only place. (adjective; Rick has just one place.)
Louie allows gambling at Rick's place only. (adverb; Of all the bars, Rick's alone is allowed to have gambling.)

Some other words that can be moved from place to place in a sentence are *just*, *merely*, *hardly*, *even*, *nearly*, and *almost*. Here are a few examples of these.

We almost lost all the transit papers. (They're all safe, but it was close.)
We lost almost all the transit papers. (Some are gone, but some are safe.)

Ingrid missed nearly all the planes. (She caught the last one, however.)
Ingrid nearly missed all the planes. (She caught them all, but it was close every time.)

Sam played just the last verse. (He skipped the others.)
Sam just played the last verse. (He finished it a moment ago.)

Peter Lorre alone can get out of town. (He's the only one who can.)
Peter Lorre can get out of town alone. (He can do it by himself.)

Remember, follow the rule for modifiers in general: a modifier must go as close as possible to the thing it modifies, and (just) moving it (just) slightly can change (just) the meaning. And remember that Bogie in fact never said, "Play it again, Sam."

I THINK; THEREFORE, I FEEL

Some words with no backbone

Have you ever been in a hot tub? You come out feeling limp and drained. Here we're going to talk about some words that have spent too much time in a hot tub; they seem soft, unable to take a firm stand and meaning.

think vs. feel How have we come to the unfortunate state of using *feel* for *think*, as in the following?

I feel that the capital of Burkina Faso is Ouagadougou. (ugh)
I think that the capital of Burkina Faso is Ouagadougou. (yes)

Using *feel* here instead of *think* makes it seem as if we are afraid to take a stand. In fact, feelings aren't even involved here. Unless you are specifically talking about feelings, go with *think*. Not "I feel that Colombo is the capital of Sri Lanka, not a TV character," but

I think that Colombo is the capital of Sri Lanka, not a TV character.

But leave *feel* in the following, because it is clearly expressing a feeling:

She felt certain that Brazzaville is the capital of the Congo and not of Gabon.

Don't be afraid to take a stand. *Think* is a good strong word; don't weaken the idea by changing it to *feel*. And don't dilute the emotional value of *feel* by using it when you mean *think*.

On a slightly different note are the following two words. Hippies gave us *relate*, and yuppies gave us *share*. The Grammar Gram would like to give both back.

relate to If you use this in speaking, the Grammar Gram promises not to get upset.

I can relate to your attitude.

The Grammar Gram won't get upset but won't be thrilled either. However, please try to avoid it in writing. It's entirely too vague. In the example, the phrase seems to mean something akin to "empathize with," but at other times it seems to mean "like": "I can relate to *Upper Volta*, the old name for Burkina Faso; it sounds as if the people are energetic." This one is better written as

I like *Upper Volta*, the old name for Burkina Faso; it sounds as if the people are energetic.

Avoid making your readers question your meaning, or attribute their own meanings to your words.

share The Grammar Gram cringes around this word, writing or speaking, because it sounds so very slimy and insincere. Of course here we're *not* talking about the word in a sentence like the following:

The residents of Tegucigalpa are always ready to share their food.

It's sentences like the following that make the Grammar Gram's skin crawl:

Thank you for sharing your feelings about Ulan Bator with us. (ugh)

The phrases *sharing that* or *sharing your feelings* are psychobabble. Sometimes we use them in response to criticism when we are trying to act like adults but we want to smack the person who said them. Instead, try this:

Thank you for telling us about your feelings.

The Grammar Gram feels that you can relate to these ideas and hopes you'll share your feelings about them.

A LITTLE PRESENT FROM THE GRAMMAR GRAM

Dear Grammar Gram:

In *Moby-Dick, does* Ahab kill the great white whale, or *did* he kill the whale?

Just call me,
Ishmael

Dear Ish:

The Grammar Gram suspects that your question is actually about tenses, specifically the "literary present"; it's not a book from your great aunt, but it is a helpful tense. More than anything, the literary present is a tense of convenience. Talking about a piece of writing, literature in particular, can get very confusing. Since all kinds of tenses may appear in a book, the tense we use to begin talking about the book is important. If we start in the past ("The whale surfaced"), our tenses can get quite complicated ("Queequeg had just finished a new tattoo when he received word that the whale had surfaced a few minutes before").

Sometimes events take place before the story begins: "After Ahab lost his leg, he got weird." References to such events must be in the past. However, to prevent confusion, start in the present and stay there as much as possible. Say, "Does Ahab kill the whale?" rather than "Did Ahab kill the whale?" Instead of "Before Ishmael signed on board the *Pequod*, he didn't have work," say,

Before Ishmael signs on board the *Pequod*, he doesn't have work.

And instead of "Ahab chased the whale into the South Atlantic," say,

Ahab chases the whale into the South Atlantic.

Even when you quote something that is in the past tense in the book, you still refer to the activity in the present:

Ishmael is surprised by Queequeg's tattoos: "[The] covered parts of him were checkered. . . ."

Once we get going, the literary present is quite easy. We just think of the story as taking place as we speak about it—as if it's going on right now. We also use the literary present to discuss the author's writing:

Melville uses the chapter called "The Whiteness of the Whale" to highlight all the bizarre and sick images associated with the color white.

But when we talk about the author as a historical figure, we still use the plain old past (or present, if the author is still alive):

Melville spent much of his life traveling in the South Seas.

This wouldn't make sense in the present tense. He's been dead for a hundred years.

The literary present applies to all writing, not only to discussions of literature. We might say, "Einstein developed [past] the Theory of Relativity," but we would say,

In his diaries, Einstein reveals [present] himself to be a sweet guy.

Read the book to find out what happens to the whale. By the way, "Ishmael" wasn't ("isn't"?) his real name.

The Grammar Gram

WHY DID YOU HIT YOUR LITTLE SISTER?

Just because

When we were little, we got away with quite a bit by answering questions such as "Why did you hit your little sister?" with statements such as "Just because." As adults, we still try to get away with that kind of thing in writing, but we need to fight against it. In using *because*, we must make the logical connection between the cause and effect as explicit as possible. We need to be aware of three don'ts:

1. Don't follow *because* with the first part of the sentence, simply reworded:
In "Siouxie and the Banshees is an odd name for a band because it's so different from other names," both halves say the same thing; no real reason is given. Such sentences are often difficult to spot because they have a sort of logical glow to them. But they just say the same thing twice. Omit "because" entirely here:

Siouxie and the Banshees is an odd name for a band; it's very different from other names.

2. Don't use *because* after the phrase *the reason is*:
"The reason she likes Ladysmith Black Mambazo is because they harmonize well." Not only is this much more complex than it needs to be, it is also redundant. A clause beginning with *because* is a reason, so we're saying it twice. Say either

The <u>reason</u> she likes Ladysmith Black Mambazo <u>is that</u> they harmonize well.

or

She likes Ladysmith Black Mambazo <u>because</u> they harmonize well.

3. Don't follow *because* with something that is actually not a reason at all:
"Alice Cooper is a great musician because he uses rats in his show." Not logical—using rats in a show doesn't make you a good musician; playing an instrument well does. Using the rats might make him a great showman but not a great musician. Since there is no logical connection here, we need a total rewrite:

Alice Cooper is a great musician. His music is enhanced by the rats he uses in his stage show.

Here's another nonreason: "The Stones' claims about the Beatles are true because my personal experience shows me they're true." The Stones' claims may be true, yes. And indeed, my personal experience may support their claims. OK so far. But this sentence says that the claims are true *because* my experience shows them to be so. Experience can only validate or support them, but it is not the reason. Let's reword the sentence:

The Stones' claims about the Beatles are validated by my personal experience.

Here's a final one in this category: "The name *Oingo Boingo* must mean something because performers spend a long time deciding on a name for their group." Again, on the surface this seems to be logical. But spending a long time deciding on a name does not mean that the name has meaning. The name means something whether or not people spent a great deal of time. We could say, however,

I hope the name *Oingo Boingo* means something, because the group spent so much time choosing it.

In closing, remember that we all need to pay attention to the word *because,* because it's worth noting. (Which rule did that sentence violate?)

BECAUSE OF THE WONDERFUL THINGS HE DOES

The Wizard of Oz and bad grammar

Bad grammar in *The Wizard of Oz*? Highly unlikely, you say? Glinda the Good Witch would have seen to it. Nonetheless, there it is in the song: "The Wizard of Oz is one . . . because of the wonderful things he does."

Because introduces a reason, a cause. And since a reason should be forceful, adhere to the following rule:

Always follow *because* with a subject and a verb.

A reason should indicate a state ("because you're green") or an activity ("because I cried"). After all, we want to provide a strong, clear reason. (And for those few of you desperate for the grammatical reason, *because* is a subordinating conjunction and therefore introduces a clause.) Let's change the song to the following:

The Wizard of Oz is one because he does wonderful things.

Now that's silly, you're saying—it doesn't clear things up, and it doesn't even rhyme. Well, perhaps. In speaking (or here, singing), we can take the liberty of being imprecise because someone can ask us what we mean; but in writing we can't afford imprecision. *Because of* is a very common form, but the actual meaning is unclear:

Dorothy was late because of the Tin Man. (no)

What does this mean? In the most general terms it does mean that the Tin Man or something connected to him made her late. But it could mean

. . . because the Tin Man was rusted.
. . . because the Tin Man was mistakenly recycled.

It's something about the Tin Man, but *because of* simply points to the general area. Of course, we might not care, but in writing we should, if only to prevent needless questions from our audience:

The wicked witch melted because of the water. (no)

Was it too hot, too alkaline? Or does water melt witches in general? If we don't know and don't care, perhaps we should reword it entirely:

The water melted the wicked witch.

Note: Don't for a minute think that you can avoid this problem by substituting *due to,* as in "We were late due to the Munchkins." It's the same problem. The question, again, is "What about the Munchkins?" They got lost? Their weird little voices finally made us crazy? What? Think of *due to* as the equivalent of *because of:* avoid them both, and find something more specific to say:

We were late because the Munchkins' very large hats caught on the scenery.

The Grammar Gram can't resist ending on a particularly terrible sentence:

The Munchkins were asked to wear smaller hats because of safety reasons. (no)

This sentence goes in a circle. "Because" equals "reasons." Perhaps it means

The Munchkins were asked to wear smaller hats because the large hats were unsafe.

It's hard, however, to get all of that out of "safety reasons." The Great and Powerful Grammar Gram has spoken (please ignore the little guy writing these Grammar Grams behind the screen).

SUBORDINATION AND HUMILIATION

Use one to prevent the other.

Some people enjoy both of these. The Grammar Gram likes to subordinate but not to humiliate. Subordinate (or "dependent") clauses are ones that can't stand by themselves as sentences. By knowing when to use a subordinate clause, we can often change the impact of a piece of writing:

Although I like a clean room, I don't like to clean.
I like a clean room, but I don't like to clean.

The meaning is basically the same, but the effect and implication are quite different in each of these. *But* indicates that both ideas are equal (see the next Grammar Gram on conjunctions) but opposite. However, *although* indicates that the main idea is "I don't like to clean" and that "I like a clean room" is less important. We can categorize subordinating words into several broad areas:

time after, as, as long as, as soon as, before, until, when, whenever, while

Please stay away until you take a shower; while I'm gone, you should shovel out your side of the room.

cause and effect because, since, so that

Please pick up all your old dinner plates so that I can get to my side.

contradiction although, though, in spite of

Although you seem like a nice person, you are, in fact, a slob from beneath the sea.

conditions unless, if

If you don't clean up, I will have to call the health department.

relative pronouns who, whom, which, that
These are slightly different. The idea they introduce is subordinate, but explains a noun or pronoun.

The slime that I'm talking about seems to be coming from your clothes, which are filthy.

QUICK RULES AND REMINDERS—AND A WARNING

1. A subordinate clause can come at the beginning, the middle, or the end of a sentence. The only consideration is the effect you are trying to achieve. Putting the clause at the beginning gives it more weight.
2. If a clause comes at the beginning, it is usually followed by a comma; if it comes at the end of a sentence, you can often omit the comma before it.
3. Be daring. Once in your life, put one clause inside another (but be careful):

I want you out because, although you have nice hair, you smell terrible.

This is more effective than "Although you have nice hair, I want you out because you smell terrible."

Note: Many of these subordinators make excellent transitions between sentences and paragraphs, too.

Because subordination is an important aspect of grammar, *while* you are working on your next piece of writing, consider using one of these words, but don't humiliate yourself.

CONJUNCTION DYSFUNCTION

And, but, or, nor, for, so, yet

Coordinating conjunctions do just what their name says: they balance (coordinating) *and* join (conjunction). The things they balance can be whole sentences: "In my telescope, I spotted a red giant, but I couldn't find a white dwarf." *Or* they can be single words or phrases: "I would settle for locating a pulsar or a quasar." *But* you know that. Let's skip right to the most interesting *and/or* difficult areas of coordination.

so Many people don't like *so* as a coordinator, so beware of it. Finding a replacement is usually easy. Instead of "The sun is a yellow dwarf now, so its next phase is as a red giant," you can say,

> Because the sun is a yellow dwarf now, its next phase is as a red giant.

Warning: "So" and "because" don't go in the same place: *because* goes with the *cause; so* goes with the *effect.* Remember, too, that using *so* creates a more mild sense of cause and effect than using *because* does. *So* equalizes the two ideas, whereas *because* introduces a less important idea. (See GRGR III.3.)

PUNCTUATING WITH COORDINATORS

Use a comma before, *not* after, the conjunction when coordinating two sentences:

> Miranda and Ariel are two of the moons of Uranus, and Charon is the moon of Pluto.

Many people are now finding it acceptable to drop the comma when the sentences are short:

> This one is a quasar and the other one is a pulsar.

The Grammar Gram thinks this is fine, as do many respectable people. *But* some don't, *so* be careful.

BEWARE OF DOUBLE COORDINATION

Double coordination most often occurs with *yet* and *so* ("and so," "but yet," "and yet"). For some reason, we don't feel comfortable with these words alone, *and so* we throw in an extra coordinator (as the Grammar Gram just did): "Globular clusters are chunky, and yet they're not candy." Using both words is redundant.

> Globular clusters are chunky, yet they're not candy.

DON'T OVERCOORDINATE

Not every idea is equal to those around it. Learn to modify and subordinate. Don't say, "Cannibal galaxies are real, and they devour other galaxies." Instead, say,

> Cannibal galaxies, which devour other galaxies, are real.

TRY STARTING A SENTENCE WITH A COORDINATOR

Yes, this is legal. Both of the following are fine:

> Miranda and Ariel are Shakespearean characters, but they are also moons of Uranus.
> Miranda and Ariel are Shakespearean characters. But they are also moons of Uranus.

When you start a sentence with a coordinator, you give it more weight than if you had just run it together.

The most obvious sin above is double coordination. *And yet* it is the most difficult to overcome.

IF AT FIRST YOU DON'T SUCCEED . . .

Revising is reseeing.

"If at first you don't succeed, try, try again" is one platitude that can help us in our writing. (Platitudes are worn-out sayings, not those little mammals with duckbills—those are platypuses.) On first drafts, we write as our thoughts come to us, and grammar and nicely formed sentences are not necessarily a part of our thought process. We write something down, and when we look at it later, it seems wrong. But we get stuck in certain grooves and can't get out of them. This Grammar Gram, then, is a reminder to rethink.

We might write something like "Who should sign the letter? You, me, or Nostradamus?" Something is wrong here: *me* isn't the right word. So we try it another way: "Who should sign the letter? You, I, or Nostradamus?" *I* is correct ("Should I sign the letter?") but sounds terrible. Here it's not only the correctness that matters but also the sound. We need to remember that it is not the first sentence itself that we want to convey but the *idea* in the first sentence. We need to go back to that idea and come up with some other versions:

Whose signature should be on the letter? Yours, mine, or Nostra's?
Should Nostradamus sign the letter? If not, should you or I sign it?

Here we simply avoid the problem in the first versions. Too often, we get distracted by one wrong or awkward phrase and forget that there are a number of correct ways. Look at the following headline from a memo: "Whom You Should Contact for Information Concerning Astral Gliding." *Whom* is grammatically correct, but *who* would probably sound better. This is a true dilemma, so take the John Wayne way out: "When the going gets tough, the tough change the sentence completely":

People to Contact for Information on Astral Gliding

Laura recently had a problem with a different kind of sentence. In a note to a friend, she said, "We'll miss your aura's not being there on the first day of school." The sentence literally says that we'll miss the "not being there." It doesn't say we'll miss the aura (which is what we assume was intended). Throw out the old forms, bring in the new:

We'll miss your aura on the first day of school.
We're sorry that your aura won't be there on the first day of school.

Sentence problems like these are very common when we are trying to avoid sexism in language: "Every student was entitled to either a palm reading or a tarot reading. Which one he or she chose was up to the individual." Ugh. Avoid "he or she"; beyond that, the sentence gets weird simply because it's the first attempt. A revision (literally, a "reseeing") clears it right up:

It was up to the individual to choose one or the other.

In another typical problem, we worry about where to put a possessive apostrophe as in "The great American yogi Meir Baba's most famous words were 'Don't worry, be happy.' " This might be OK, but we really want to make *yogi* possessive. If we don't know what to do, we avoid the problem entirely:

The most famous words of the great American yogi Meir Baba were "Don't worry, be happy."

No possessives there to trip us up. (And no, Bobby McFerrin didn't say those words first.) We need to remember that we're trying to convey an idea and that there are a variety of ways to construct a sentence/that we can construct a sentence in a variety of ways/that most sentences can be constructed in several different ways/that there is no one way to construct a sentence, although there might be a best way.

JEOPARDY!

Please don't phrase your answer in the form of a question.

Sometimes when we ask a question in our writing, we try to set it up as follows: "Therefore, we must ask, who is the greatest female figure skater?" But this won't do. The sentence starts as a statement and ends as a question. That little comma after *ask* isn't enough to introduce the question. At the very least here, we need to make the last part into a real question, with quotation marks and all, as if it were someone else's question:

Therefore, we must ask, "Who is the greatest female figure skater?"

This is fine, but sometimes it may seem a little odd to set up our own questions this way. We do have an alternative; we can turn such a question into an *indirect question*:

Therefore, we must ask who the greatest female figure skater is.

An indirect question like this one is actually a quite simple way of conveying the idea of a question without having to jump through all the hoops often required of a question. Since we form a question by putting the verb before the subject, in an indirect question we simply move the verb back to its regular place after the subject.

Different kinds of questions demand different kinds of indirect questions. We will outline some of the various kinds and underline the significant changes.

Salima wondered, "Was Sonja Henie the greatest figure skater?"
Salima wondered whether Sonja Henie was the greatest figure skater.

The question is, "Can we ignore Katarina Witt and Peggy Fleming?"
The question is whether we can ignore Katarina Witt and Peggy Fleming.

Eduardo asked, "How could they forget about Dorothy Hamill?"
Eduardo asked how they could forget about Dorothy Hamill.

Debi Thomas asked me, "Do you skate every day?"
Debi Thomas asked me whether I skate every day.

"Would you skate with Tiffany Chin?" they asked Dick Button.
They asked Dick Button if he would skate with Tiffany Chin.

It should be clear that indirect questions are not only appropriate for our own thoughts, but also for quotations. Sometimes a quotation doesn't fit with what we are trying to do; in such a case, we can paraphrase the quotation and turn it into an indirect question.

Finally, be aware that tenses must often change when you switch from a direct to an indirect question, as the following examples show:

"I have wanted to skate all my life," she told *Ice* magazine.
She told *Ice* magazine that she had wanted to skate all her life.

The reason for changes such as this one is that if we aren't quoting, all tenses must match. The sentence in the example starts in the past (*told*), and if something happened before that past, it must be in the past perfect (*had wanted*). Don't worry about what these tenses are called, but do check to make sure they are correct.

Now that we're done, the Grammar Gram wants to know, "Did you learn something?" Now that we're done, the Grammar Gram wants to know whether you learned something.

IS THIS A GOOD GRAMMAR GRAM, OR WHAT?

Rhetorical questions

Few of us remember what the term *rhetorical* means. We've come to think of it as meaning "empty" or "meaningless," and a rhetorical question becomes a question that we know the answer to. Thus we say, "Oh, that's just a rhetorical question." But rhetoric is the art of persuasion, and a rhetorical question is anything but empty or meaningless. Its very purpose is to persuade or to aid us in persuading. There are two kinds of rhetorical questions.

1. Questions that need no answer:

Doesn't the sun shine on us all, mollusk and crustacean alike?

Of course it does. This is the kind of question that simply reminds us of a truth, and so needs no answer. Often such a general truth disguised as a question is a good way to provoke us into thinking about some larger issue: in this case, perhaps the equality of the orders of invertebrates. Here's a slightly different one:

How long must arthropods suffer these indignities?

In fact, there is no answer for such a question. But it should make us think.

2. Questions with an answer implied in the context:

Should any arachnid (mentally stable or not) who wants one be allowed to have a gun?

Even though the answer at first seems as if it should be "No, not all spiders should be allowed to carry firearms," we are really guessing unless we have the context. If the question were being posed by the NARA (National Arachnid Rifle Association), the answer might well be "Yes, because the Constitution guarantees us this right." But from the context, we will know without hesitation.

Caution: *Overusing rehtorical questions is hazardous.* Rhetorical questions are wonderful, but too many of them are indeed too much of a good thing:

The invertebrates are beings, too, aren't they? They live and breathe. Why should they be denied basic rights: a job, a home, a roundworm in every claw? If we treat them as less than ourselves, aren't we sinking to the level of animals or worse?

Well, you get the idea. Remember that rhetorical questions are not so much questions as they are persuasive techniques; here they aren't persuading. Pick the strongest; junk the others.

Note: Although rhetorical questions don't need an answer, in fact we sometimes answer them for the same reason we ask them: to create a mood that will persuade:

Should a hermit crab be denied a snail shell for a home? Never.

TAG QUESTIONS

Tag questions are little questions tacked onto the end of a statement, usually as a way of getting your reader to confirm what you've just said. Sometimes we use them to force a response; other times we use them because we're insecure. They are more frequently used in speaking, but they do occur in writing:

This has been a thought-provoking Grammar Gram, hasn't it?

THE CAMELOPARD SENTENCE

Sentences that are half statement and half question

Dear Grammar Gram:

Sometimes when I write, I like to ask my reader a question or two, but do you think it's OK to have a question and a statement together? Does it sound awkward, because if it does, I won't do it.

Signed,
Just Asking

Dear Asking:

Yes and no. Look at your own last sentence. Since there's a question there, you might want a question mark. But where? Certainly not at the end of the sentence, because the last part is not a question, and it wouldn't make sense. Certainly not after *awkward*, because then you would have a question mark all by itself in the middle of a sentence. Out of these ideas, we can construct Rule 1:

A sentence can't begin with a question and end with a statement.

What should you do with your sentence, then? Reword the first part or divide it into two sentences:

If it sounds awkward, then I won't do it.
Does it sound awkward? If it does, I won't do it.

This one has been quite easy to fix because the only real problem was that we were recording spoken English. However, sometimes, especially when we get all fired up, we might write something like this:

We want her penned because why should pandas be allowed to panhandle?

Here the first part is fine: *We want her penned.* Then we see *because*, and we expect a reason to follow. Instead, we get a rhetorical question. To eliminate the awkwardness make the second part just a statement:

We want her penned because pandas shouldn't be allowed to panhandle.

From this we can develop Rule 2:

A reason cannot be a question.

So when can we combine statements and questions? Here's an example:

We want An-An to go to Panama, but will she create pandemonium there?

A question may follow a statement if the two are closely related. Here the question grows out of the statement. It's like saying "We want An-An to go to Panama, but we're afraid she'll create pandemonium there."

Finally, a question can be part of a conditional statement if the question follows logically:

If she's the only panda I know, then why shouldn't I pander to her?

The Grammar Gram forgot to mention it, but did you know that a *camelopard* is what people used to call a giraffe because it looked like half leopard and half camel? (Would you change that last sentence?)

The Grammar Gram

LET'S GET THIS BABY OFF THE GROUND

Six rules to help you get going

Even people with the most important things in the world to say find it difficult to get going. One of the saddest things to the Grammar Gram (next to the Chicago Cubs) is to see someone with good ideas produce a poor piece of work because the person spent too much time on the introduction. This brings us to our rules.

1. For any kind of writing, scribble down a tentative introduction simply to get yourself writing. Don't work on it very much. You may want to change it later, because you actually won't know what you'll be introducing until you write it. If you haven't written the rest of the paper, report, exam, or memo, how do you know what it is you're introducing? If you're in an essay exam, you might even consider leaving the first few lines blank, so you can write the introduction after you've written the essay. Don't laugh at this rule until you've tried it.

2. The best introduction will do at least three things: it will set the tone of your piece of writing; it will lay out the problem, or begin to lay it out; and it will give the reader some general direction.

3. You do not have to give everything away in the opening. You do not have to say, "In this paper, I will first give some background on puff adders, then I will discuss the pros and cons of keeping them as pets, and I will end with a recommendation." In fact, in short pieces, most readers will thank you profusely if you don't give away too much. Some first paragraphs are very brief; witness the following, the opening paragraph from an essay by Lewis Thomas:

> Insects again.

4. Do not make yourself the focus of the introduction, unless you are the focus of the paper or report. That is, try to avoid, "I will discuss . . . ," "I will first . . . ," "I hope to prove . . . ," and the like. If you say, "I believe that chihuahuas should not live in apartments," the main part of the sentence is "I believe." The reader's focus is then on you and your beliefs, not on chihuahuas. Avoiding these phrases, however, does not give you permission to use the passive: "Three things will be discussed." That's cheating. You must force yourself to think of other options, such as "The three things most important to our discussion are. . . ."

5. Be selective about what you put in your introduction. Sometimes you may be tempted to start with background and end up overdoing it:

> Since the beginning of the industrial revolution, poodle labor has been a source of controversy. Poodle labor laws, while they have greatly reduced abuses of poodles, have not altogether solved the problems. Poodles working in the family store, for instance, ... [and on and on and on]. All this leads us to a vital question: who will care for our poodles?

Why not start with the question—"Who will care for our poodles?"—and provide the background later, perhaps in another paragraph? Now the first thing we read will certainly grab our attention.

6. When beginning letters and memos, don't try too hard. Phrases like these work just fine:

> This letter is to confirm . . .
> As you may know, every year . . .
> To follow up on our discussion last week, I . . .
> Thank you for your note. However, I must . . .

The main thing is to get going as soon as possible. And do what you would do for any other piece of writing: lay out what you're going to talk about and pay attention to tone.

IN THE BEGINNING WAS THE WORD

"Ninety-nine percent of pieces of writing fail in the first three sentences."—A famous grammar guru

You probably can't top the opening words of the Bible for impact, but you can do a number of things to make your opening work for you. The opening of a piece of writing can be like the first moments of an airline flight. You grab hold of the armrests, clench your teeth, and hope that you won't crash on takeoff. To prevent both the crash and the fear of the crash, this Grammar Gram gives you some things to grab onto, things that will also grab your reader. The very first words also set the snooze level for your audience. If you open with a boring statement, your reader will have a nice nap. But look what happens when you use other kinds of openings.

An anecdote "When George Bernard Shaw was on the train from Paris to Rome, the woman seated next to him said, 'Sir, you smell.' 'No, madam,' he replied, 'You smell. I stink.' " Now you have the reader's attention.

A quotation See the one at the beginning of this Grammar Gram. The quotation should be directly relevant. It can be indented and separated from the body of the paper. Be sure to cite the source.

A statistic An essay on fancy bottled drinking water might begin with the following, which can be indented like a quotation: "The Mississippi drainage basin is the third largest in the world." Then the first sentence of the paper might be "With so much water of our own, one wonders why Americans have to buy it from France."

A startling statement or fact "The male *Acarophenax tribolii* mite mates with its sisters inside the mother, then dies before it is born." Perhaps just the thing for a paper on feminism.

A question "Why do we fear speaking in public more than death itself?"

A generalization "When a fine book gets made into a movie, it almost always loses something in the transition." The beauty of such a generalization is that either side can follow: "The movie version of *Candy* is an exception" or "The movie version of *Candy* is no exception."

A problem or a dilemma "When the clerk at the grocery store says, 'Paper or plastic?' how should we answer? That plastic bag will last for a million years, perhaps; on the other hand, that paper bag might mean the death of a tree two hundred years old."

A single word (so it better be good) " 'Dentist.' The very word makes my teeth hurt and my palms sweat."

Every piece of writing is unique: you can't necessarily start every essay with a quotation or every report with a startling statistic. Choose the opening that best suits your needs. And please note that the Grammar Gram has a hard and fast rule. If you begin with a quotation, a statistic, or some other attention grabber, you must refer to it immediately; don't let it hang there at the beginning without comment. In addition, you must use it in the course of your piece of writing: use it as a theme, perhaps, or come back to it at the end.

Note: Though we *read* an opening first, we don't always write it first. Some people agonize over a clever opening so much that the rest of the piece suffers. Sometimes you write the opening last—once you know what you'll be talking about.

Although 99 percent of pieces of writing may fail in the first three sentences, yours can succeed if you pay attention to this Grammar Gram. (Note how cleverly the Grammar Gram refers to the opening here at the end.)

MAY I TAKE YOUR ORDER, PLEASE?

Please read this Grammar Gram by following the numbers.

2. Beware of these dangerous words and phrases. "*The first thing* I want to talk about . . ."; "*Another way* we use. . . ." Although these terms are good when used accurately, they are often symptoms that you are not creating an order for your writing. Often they indicate a random list of ideas. Therefore, your first task is to

4. Consider ordering by chronology. Kinds of writing: lab reports, scientific papers, narrative essays, and articles on history. Indicator words: *beginning, next, after, the first thing, before, finally.*

5. Some ideas are best put in order of importance. Kinds of writing: argumentative essays, lists of demands, articles on social problems. Indicator words: *least, most, we can disregard, we cannot ignore.* The most important point usually (but not always) will come last because you want people to remember it. A piece of writing that ends with a minor point is like a cartoon shown after, rather than before, the movie.

1. In any piece of writing, from essays to memos to reports, some subjects demand a certain order. A piece of writing can fail simply because the writer didn't pay attention to the order. Writing teachers hate to ask, "Why did you put paragraph three where it is instead of after paragraph five?" because they know that the answer is often "I don't know." Let's start with some words to avoid:

3. Decide on an order. Sometimes the order is obvious (for example, in a recipe); at other times you must decide which order is best for your argument. Various kinds of writing work well with particular kinds of organization. Notice that the words that help to indicate that order are also among the words you use for transitions at the beginnings and ends of sentences and paragraphs.

6. The possibilities for organizing are not limited to the "big two" (points 4 and 5); they are limitless:
Complexity or difficulty: "The easiest way to skin a cat is . . ."
Qualifications: "Of the candidates, Ferraro is the most qualified . . ."
Pain or anger: "What hurts the most is . . ."
Silliness: "The most ridiculous aspect . . ."

8. In our sample paragraph, we start with the most obvious (one last drive), but it is also the least important here. Then we move to the next most obvious (businesses closing) and slightly more important. Then to more important (people cleaning their cars). And we end with the idea that is the least obvious (that they'll just sit in their driveways reminiscing) but the most important. The same can be done in an essay.

7. In any order, we can move either direction, depending on what we want. If we order by size, we can start with either the largest or the smallest, depending on where we want the paper to end. Rarely, however, do we organize in just one way. What's the order in the following paragraph?

> What would happen if we knew that beginning tomorrow, all cars would disappear from the earth? Of course, most people would probably want to take one last drive, which would create massive traffic jams. Dealerships, repair shops, and auto supply stores would probably be closed, but carwashes might do a booming business as people lovingly clean and wax their cars one more time. Most likely, though, people will spend those last hours sitting in their cars in the driveway, dreaming of all the fun they had on the road, at the drive-in, or just around town.

9. If the Grammar Gram had considered the order to begin with, this would have been easier to read.

REPENT, FOR THE END IS NEAR

How to begin to conclude a piece of writing

When it comes to announcing the end of a piece of writing, there are four kinds of writers. Some just can't seem to stop, and we tune out before they turn off. Others stop suddenly: we turn the page to see what is coming up and it's blank; we're surprised and a little embarrassed, as if we're saying, "But officer, I didn't see it coming!" A very few writers let us know that the end is coming and then end right where they should. But most of us just meander on to the ending—we get there, but not as well as we could with a little thought. Everything we do should be leading up to our ending: the ideas should build one on another so that the ending, when it comes, shows up at just the right time. Here are a few ways to announce the end.

TO SUMMARIZE OR NOT TO SUMMARIZE?

The last paragraph need not be a summary of the paper. In longer scientific papers, learned articles, and reports, a summary is necessary, but not in shorter pieces. The following words are OK—but just OK:

In conclusion   To conclude   In sum   In summary

These all suffer from a writer's disease called Let-me-hit-the-reader-over-the-head-itis. In its severest manifestation, it takes the form of "In this paper, I have discussed. . . ." Before using that phrase, consider changing professions. We want to know we're at the conclusion because things are falling into place, not because the writer has held up a big sign that says, "Slow to 15 words per minute. Paper about to end." But a summary conclusion can be done well, as in the following:

Cabbage, as we have seen, is neither good nor bad. It's how we use it that counts.

Notice that this summary doesn't use the word *summary* or *conclusion* or any variation.

OTHER END MOVES

There are as many good endings as there are good pieces of writing. Following are a few ways to begin the final paragraph; the underlined words indicate that the end is near.

Loose ends tied together or pieces falling into place:

The bulk of the evidence, then, indicates that cabbage is not a virus from space.
Having examined all these factors, we can determine that cabbage is native to earth.

The major point of the paper:

The most compelling aspect of the space virus theory is its simplicity.

A final jab at the opposition:

Considering all the facts we have mustered, it's amazing that some people still adhere to the cabbage-as-mutant-brussels-sprout theory.

The beginning of a broader perspective:

Although we are rightly suspicious of cabbage, we should look at it historically.

Each approach introduces the end of the paper in a different way, but all do so clearly without announcing the fact in headlines. Remember, the last paragraph is our last chance—how we begin that paragraph is important.

FAMOUS LAST WORDS

How to conclude a piece of writing

In the previous Grammar Gram, we talked about how to get into the conclusion. Now let's talk about how to get out of the conclusion. Unfortunately, we can't end a piece of writing as Porky Pig does in Looney Tunes cartoons just by writing "That's all, folks!" And we can't end it as a movie director does by yelling "Cut!" or "It's a wrap." We need something more.

Final words are important. Often they are what the reader will remember. What will those final words be? Will they be memorable, like those spoken by Beethoven (who was deaf, remember): "I shall hear in heaven"? Or will the paper just dribble away? Some of the good things that we use to begin an essay we can also use to end one, for instance:

A quotation Introduce it in the last sentence ("As Yogi Berra said, 'It's déjà vu all over again.' ") or space it from the last paragraph and center it on the page. Once in your life, you may also twist a famous quotation; a paper on the liquor industry might end with "As Dorothy Parker almost said, 'Candy is dandy, but liquor is where the money is.' "

A question At the end of a piece of writing, sometimes a rhetorical question will work, such as "Can we doubt, then, that lima beans are legumes from hell?" The question must grow naturally out of the paper.

A generalization You have completed a paper showing that the good novel *Day of the Triffids* was made into a terrible movie. Move from the single novel-to-movie saga you've talked about to the larger issue of translating a book to film. The final line of the paper, then, might be "When a fine book gets made into a movie, it almost always loses something in the transition."

A look to the future A paper on the explosive growth in the tribble population might end with "As things stand now, we are not in terrible trouble with tribbles, but in ten years, we may be."

Your hopes This is actually a subset of the look to the future: "We can only hope that some day parents will see the foolishness of naming their children after major appliances."

A call for action This doesn't always have to sound like "Workers of the world unite; you have nothing to lose but your chains" (although that is a snappy ending). It can be milder, as in "Next time you feel a fast-food feeding frenzy coming on, reach for a carrot instead. The image of those fries will fade in time; but the grease won't."

Occasionally, several techniques will work together at the end. For instance, a look to the future (complete with statistic) might be followed by a question: "Broccoli will account for half our vegetable intake by the year 2050. Will we be prepared?" Do be careful, though. Too many different techniques will make you sound like an idiot.

The key to all these endings is that they serve in a concise way not only to stop the reader but also to summarize what has been said. The last words of the great French novelist André Gide were not irrelevant to his life: "I'm afraid," he said, "my sentences are becoming ungrammatical." Don't work any harder on the ending, however, than on the opening (or the middle, for that matter). The ending just gets us out; it can't save an otherwise poor piece of writing.

Let's end with the ways *not* to end a piece of writing. Don't end with "The End" (even if you say it in French or Spanish or Chinese). Finally, remember that those little dots called ellipses are used primarily to indicate that something has been left out of a quotation, so don't end with . . .

THE THEORY OF RELATIVITY

Dear Grammar Gram:

Someone recently told me that the theory of relativity had to do with paragraph size. I always thought the theory had to do with energy and mass and the speed of light. Now I'm upset. Is nothing constant in this world?

Signed,
Albert E.

Dear Bert:

Do you by any chance have messy hair and did you date Marilyn Monroe? Never mind. The theory of relativity in writing simply states that the size of a paragraph in relation to those around it tells us the relative importance of that paragraph. Usually, the bigger the paragraph, the more important it will be. First let's develop a few simple rules, and then the Grammar Gram will show you a nice, scientific-looking diagram.

1. There is such a thing as too big a paragraph. Paragraphs on a page make us feel that we can pause if we want to; a whole page without breaks is not appealing.

2. One sentence may be a paragraph. But that's usually true only if the paragraph is acting as a transition:

> We have seen that ear size is not related to intelligence, but we must wonder whether big toe circumference doesn't play some role in mathematical ability.

3. In relatively short pieces, the introductory and concluding paragraphs should not be very long.

4. Varying the size of paragraphs is a way of keeping the audience with you. The size of a paragraph should depend on the ideas; it would be an odd coincidence if all the ideas and paragraphs in a piece of writing were the same size.

Looking at the relative sizes of paragraphs will help you get a sense of how a piece of writing is working. Following are the relative paragraph sizes from four different short essays.

The essay on the far left is the superior one here. It has a brief introduction and conclusion, two major paragraphs, and one smaller one, perhaps a transition between the two major ideas.

Now find a piece of your own writing and plot the relative sizes.

The Grammar Gram

THE SPACE-TIME CONTINUUM

If it's so unimportant, why did you spend three paragraphs on it?

Here is one of the few grammar jokes in existence:

> A young man from Kansas has entered Harvard as a freshman. His parents had emigrated from Norway and started a hog farm. He got accustomed to people making jokes about pigs. He was able to develop a thick skin and to learn not to let other people make his life miserable. In his first week at Harvard, he's wandering around campus and he's lost. He's wearing his little freshman beanie, so people know he's new. He approaches an upperclassman and says, "Excuse me, sir, could you tell me where the library is at?" The upperclassman glares at him, with the glare only some snob from Short Hills could muster, and says, "Pardon me. I don't know what backwoods town you come from, but here at Harvard, we don't end our sentences with prepositions." The poor boy from Kansas is very embarrassed at first but quickly regains his composure and says, "Please, let me try again. Excuse me, could you tell me where the library is at, jerk-face?"

While much of a joke is in the telling, here we have information that turns out to be misleading. It actually doesn't matter that the young man is from Kansas, that his parents are immigrants, that the upperclassman is from Short Hills. But it's the kind of information that readers register because we think it will be important. Then we feel robbed because it has nothing to do with the point. Here's a shorter version of the joke:

> A new freshman at Harvard is lost. He approaches an upperclassman and says, "Excuse me, could you tell me where the library is at?" The upperclassman glares at him and says, "Here at Harvard, we don't end our sentences with prepositions." "Then let me try again," the freshman replies. "Excuse me, could you tell me where the library is at, jerk-face?"

Out of this, let's develop a rule: the more space you spend on a topic (and hence the more time a reader must spend on it), the more important the topic probably is. As in the first version of the joke, sometimes we do devote more time to something than it deserves. Of course, the opposite is also true. Sometimes we don't devote enough time, as in the following story:

> Too many people were lingering at one of P. T. Barnum's exhibits once, so he put up a sign that said, "To the egress," and they all left.

An appropriate response to this story would be "Huh?" In fact, all the basics are here, but something is missing. Let's fill in a bit:

> P. T. Barnum was a master of manipulation. Once he found that one of his exhibits was too popular; people were lingering too long, and he was losing money because he couldn't move them through fast enough. Suddenly he thought of the solution. He put up a big sign, pointing to the rear door, that said, "To the egress." People moved quickly through the exhibit, eager to see what an egress looked like. Once outside, they probably realized that an egress is just an exit.

Now it's a story that makes sense. "But sometimes a minor point in my paper might be quite complex," you say, "so I will have to devote time to it." No. Nope. Naw. If it's truly minor, you need to cut down on it. If you can't, it is probably more important than you think. Then you must make some hard choices about what to include and what to omit. Try putting it in a footnote or an appendix; they are perfect places to stash ideas that you don't want to lose but don't want to put in the body of a piece of writing.

This Way to the Egress ⟹

CONCESSION STANDS

Git yer hot dogs, sodas, opposing arguments.

As readers, we like to feel that what we're reading is logical and carefully constructed. As writers, we can reinforce the sense of logic and care in construction by using a concession. We will not be selling popcorn in this concession; we will be admitting (conceding) that the opposing argument has some merit.

WHY GIVE UP SOMETHING TO THE OTHER SIDE?

First, we want to demonstrate that we have thought the issues through and see both sides. Second, if we agree to some aspect, the reader is less apt to try to find the weakness in our argument. Third, the concession can actually show the strength of our own argument. It's like spotting your great-aunt ten points at playing table tennis. You're probably going to win, but you've helped the other side a little.

WHAT DOES A CONCESSION LOOK LIKE?

A concession clause will probably begin with *although* or a word that acts like it, often as part of a thesis:

> Although they do provide much-needed jobs in the area, the vast pasta ranches of central Montana hurt the environment more than strip mining does.

This paper will be on the negative effects of the famous Montana pasta ranches, but the writer is conceding that the ranches do provide employment. We may want to develop this concession in a paragraph:

> The economy of the area is depressed, and the ranches do provide work for the large population of Norwegian bachelor farmers. These "Bjorns," as they are called, are ideal workers on the ranches: their familiarity with starches and carbohydrates allows them to adapt easily to working with the various pastas, from the hearty lasagna to the more sensitive rigatoni.

Now we turn to our own argument. (Note that the concession paragraph can't begin with the concession clause; it must expand on the idea in the clause.) The next paragraph might begin as follows:

> It is the very sensitivity of some of the pastas, however, that is the problem. The pastas must be rotated regularly, or they deplete the soil of all nutrients.

Immediately, then, we have turned the concession to our advantage as we begin our argument.

WHAT ARE THE KEY WORDS?

To be sure, of course, we can agree that, sometimes, often, admittedly—such words signal to the reader that we assent to some of the opposition's ideas.

WHERE DOES A CONCESSION APPEAR IN A PAPER?

It must appear near the beginning, often best right after the introduction. If we end a paper with a concession, the reader may say, "My, that's a good idea; I like it better than those I've seen in the rest of the paper."

ARE THERE PITFALLS?

Beware of a false concession, like the following: "Although many people believe that slurping macaroni is disgusting, I think it isn't." We are not giving up anything here, just pointing out that there are two sides.

Although some people don't believe in concessions, the Grammar Gram does. (Is that a true concession?)

BEING DRIVEN TO ABSTRACTION

On a concrete highway

Concrete words (*chair, tongue, floppy disk*) rarely confuse the reader; abstract words (*heaven, curiosity, disgust*) are open to interpretation. The difference between these two kinds of words is like the difference between a symphony and a country/western song. We listen to a symphony and say, "Here I think the composer is feeling despair." We listen to a country song and know exactly what the lyrics mean: "I'm taking the dog and leaving the double-wide mobile home to you."

WHEN TO BE ABSTRACT

Sometimes we want to make our readers draw their own conclusions. For example, by saying, "When love is gone, there's always justice; and when justice is gone, there's always force," performance artist and singer Laurie Anderson forces us to our own interpretation; after all, *love, justice* and *force* mean something different to each person. Such images can work in prose as well as poetry.

However, we usually want our readers to know exactly what we mean; so we want to be as concrete as possible.

The more abstract the topic, the more concrete the discussion

How should we talk about such things as understanding, knowledge, perception, and time? We should take our lead from the philosopher George Berkeley, who used tulips, houses, rocks, mites' feet, and a squirrel hiding behind a tree to discuss some of those very abstract philosophical issues.

Reduce the abstraction to the appropriate level

Being more concrete often also means being more specific:

mental activity ⇒ negative emotion ⇒ hatred ⇒ hatred of okra ⇒ gagging every time you eat it

The level you will choose depends on the topic and the audience. "Mental activity" might be used in a philosophy paper; "gagging on okra" is probably best for a personal experience essay.

Use active sentences and concrete words, with people as the subjects

Don't say, "Reality is determined solely by visual stimulus." Say instead,

If we see something, that thing is real.

Use analogies, metaphors, and similes

Rambo used one of the best metaphors for explaining a difficult idea: "I am your worst nightmare."

Use examples

Using examples is one of the best ways to make abstract ideas more concrete and clear:

Jealousy can become all-consuming. What starts out as a tinge of resentment at your best friend's promotion, for example, can slowly, insidiously become a rage so deep that you cannot sleep.

This Grammar Gram has a rare guest conclusion, by C. S. Lewis: "If you tell me something is a pleasure, I don't know whether it is more like revenge, or buttered toast, or success, or adoration, or relief from danger, or a good scratch."

EVIDENCE

How do we know that the can contains spinach, Mr. Popeye?

Just like Perry Mason or the folks on *L.A. Law*, we must adhere to certain levels of proof and evidence in all writing. We will focus here on writing about literature, but the principles apply to writing in general. Legal classifications of evidence provide helpful analogies for understanding the kinds of evidence we use in writing.

1. Direct evidence. This consists of explicit proof from the text, usually in the form of the words of an omniscient narrator (the kind who knows everyone's thoughts). (If a piece is written in the first person, that is, using *I*, then we can't always implicitly trust the narrator; the narrator is telling a personal story and may have motives we don't see.) In philosophy, direct evidence is called *empirical evidence*. Here's an example:

Popeye wasn't able to reach his spinach can in time.

We can use such a statement as a fact. It's laid out without qualification, so we can believe it. If the omniscient narrator makes such a statement, we have no choice but to believe it.

2. Hearsay evidence. In this kind of evidence, a character will assert that something happened or that someone said something, but as readers, we won't know that as fact:

Olive Oyl said, "Popeye yelled obscenities at the big brute."

That may be true, but unless the omniscient narrator said it, we can only take it as hearsay. An attorney building a case cannot base an entire argument on this evidence alone, and neither can we as writers: it's too weak.

3. Circumstantial evidence. This indirect evidence often refers to the result of an action or some other aspect of a story but does not show us the action itself:

Bluto showed up with a black eye.

By itself, this is not enough to convict Popeye of assault and battery, but if we add more circumstantial evidence ("Popeye's hand hurt") and perhaps combine it with the hearsay from Ms. Oyl, what we have is a pretty good case that Popeye is not quite the nice guy he appears to be and probably did hit Bluto.

4. Evidence by analogy or by character analysis. These are the weakest kinds of evidence; by themselves they may not prove anything, but we can use them to support our case. Evidence by analogy relies on our own experience, on our remembering how other characters or people act in similar situations: "In study after study, cartoon characters who find themselves in Popeye's position often resort to violence." Evidence by character analysis depends on our ability to see whether the particular action fits in with the larger attributes of the character: is Popeye, for instance, the kind of guy to hit someone for no reason?

THE WORDS WE USE

The kind of evidence we have tells us the kinds of words we can use. Direct evidence allows us to say, "Popeye attacked Bluto unmercifully," whereas a single piece of circumstantial or hearsay evidence may allow us to say only, "There is the possibility that . . . " or "Perhaps . . . " Combinations of hearsay and circumstantial evidence will allow us to make stronger and stronger statements, like "It seems that . . . " or "Popeye most probably . . . " In talking about literature, we can safely assert that things happened if we can muster the appropriate circumstantial and hearsay evidence.

How, then, do we know that the can contains spinach?

TWO, FOUR, SIX, EIGHT, WHAT DO WE APPRECIATE?

I appreciate your calling; I don't appreciate you whining, however.

Is the "correct" (and the Grammar Gram uses the term loosely) form "I appreciate you calling" or "I appreciate your calling"? Here the correct form is "I appreciate your calling" (and "I don't appreciate your whining, however").

Why? Look at what is being said. What do I appreciate? Do I appreciate you? Well, of course I do. But not in this sentence. What is it then? I appreciate an act—the act of calling—so I appreciate *your* calling.

But (there always is one, you know) not all *ing* forms need a possessive pronoun:

Didn't I see you biting your fingernails during a meeting?

I saw you, first of all. Then I saw you performing an activity (a disgusting one, at that).

A pair of tests will help you determine whether you should use *you* or *your.* Test 1: turn the *ing* word (the verbal) into a noun. Test 2: eliminate the verbal altogether. Trying one or both of these should reveal the correct version.

Test 1 applied to the first sentence above: "I appreciate your call." It works this way, so use *your.* Now try it on the second example: "Didn't I see you . . . "—the Grammar Gram can't think of a noun that will work, even if we change *you* to *your.* Since it doesn't work, apply Test 2: "Didn't I see you during a meeting?" It makes sense. But Test 2 wouldn't work with the first example: "I appreciate you." The whole meaning is changed. Conclusion: Use *your* if it's the activity you're interested in and *you* if it's the person.

These tests work not only with *your,* but with other pronouns (and usually nouns) as well:

The president didn't take kindly to my sitting on her desk. (not *me sitting*—it was the act, not the person, she didn't like—I hope)

Fritz loved to watch mice. All day long he looked forward to their *reproducing.* (not them reproducing because he liked their activity more than the mice)

The collapse of the university can be attributed to the bell tower's toppling over on the dean's picnic. (not the tower itself, but what it did)

The vice president in charge of money shouldn't sing. I should know; I heard him singing in the shower. (What would "I heard his singing in the shower" mean?)

Let's end with some quickies that, as they say, go both ways:

I can't stand his singing. (He's got a terrible voice.)
I can't stand him singing. (That Pavarotti's got a good voice, but he insists on singing while I'm trying to talk.)

I appreciate you reading this. (I was afraid I might have to.)
I appreciate your reading this. (Thanks for taking the time.)

If you're desperate for more punishment, your looking up *gerunds* and *participles* in a grammar book may provide details.

THIS YAM IS YOUR YAM, THIS YAM IS MY YAM

Problems with possessives and a tribute to Yma Sumac

We all know how to form possessives. And we know when to use them. Sometimes we just add an apostrophe (the Perkins' poodle) or an apostrophe and an *s* (William's warts), or sometimes we use the possessive pronoun (this is *your* artichoke). And we generally know how to use possessives:

This is my yam. This is Yma's yam. (no problem)
This yam is mine. This yam is Yma's. (no problem)

ONE YAM, TWO OWNERS

Sometimes possessives trip us up when they come in pairs. What if Yma and I own the yam together? When the possessives come after the noun *yam*, they work fine:

This yam is Yma's and mine.

When we use one pronoun and one noun, the noun needs to be made possessive (otherwise we would be saying, "This yam is Yma"). The possessive pronoun doesn't provide the needed *s* ending. If we put the possessives before the noun, things get stickier. Can we say, "This is Yma's and my yam"? Yes, we can, but it sounds rotten, so why bother? In this case, we're better off changing it to read,

This yam belongs to Yma and me.

If we are using two possessive nouns instead of pronouns, we can drop the *s* on the first one when they have joint custody. We treat the two, Eunice and Yma, as if they are one unit. The *s* on the second one makes the whole group possessive:

This is Eunice and Yma's yam. This yam is Eunice and Yma's. These are Eunice and Yma's yams.

TWO YAMS, TWO OWNERS

If they have separate yams, both nouns need to be possessive:

These are Eunice's and Yma's yams. These yams are Eunice's and Yma's.

OTHER PROBLEMS

It's not just *my* and *mine* that trip us up. Other pronouns can cause problems, too:

This is Eunice's and our yam.

This is correct but ugly. When the going gets awkward, the awkward gets dropped. Rewrite:

This yam belongs to Eunice and us.

Finally, we sometimes want to make incorrect an already correct but terrible sentence. "This is your and my yam" is correct, but the temptatation is so say, "This is yours and my yam." As always, better to avoid the problem:

This yam belongs to you and me.

Who is Yma Sumac? Known as the "Inca Princess," she was a popular singer in the 1950s. Some people think that her name is "Amy Camus" spelled backward, but the secret will always be *hers* and *her manager's.*

ME, MYSELF, AND I

May the grammar doctor check your reflexives?

If you've been paying attention to your Grammar Grams, you know that *I* is always a subject: "I think the ulna is my favorite bone."

You also know that *me* is always an object: "The femur, however, bores me."

But what about *myself* and its pals *yourself, himself, herself, themselves, ourselves,* and *itself*? The Grammar Gram is willing to bet that you're a little unsure of when to use them and may not even know that they are called *reflexive pronouns*. In fact, many people are guilty of using them incorrectly, as in the following: "Either you, Tran, or myself should keep those old kneecaps someplace dry." The word should be *I* instead of *myself* because it is a subject:

Either you, Tran, or I should keep those old kneecaps someplace dry.

We make this mistake because *myself* has a formal ring to it; it sounds more correct sometimes, but in cases like this, it's not. Here it's in the category of hyperurbanisms (see GRGR VIII.2 in the original *Grammar Grams*). In fact, the use of *myself* in these situations makes our writing not only wrong but also stuffy. Let's look at one more: "Give that box of shoulder blades to Kyoko or myself." Here the word should be *me* because it's an object:

Give that box of shoulder blades to Kyoko or me.

In spite of the little problems we have using them, *myself* and the other reflexive pronouns actually have quite clear uses. The first use is for emphasis:

I myself don't think that the shinbone is connected to the thighbone.

By adding *myself*, the writer is simply emphasizing the personal nature of the statement; in fact, a good way to test this use is to see whether you can substitute the word *personally*. If you can, a reflexive pronoun is probably acceptable:

The curator herself examines all sternums we ship.

The curator personally examines all sternums we ship.

The most common correct use of a reflexive pronoun is in a sentence in which the subject and the object are the same thing:

The scientists embarrassed themselves by putting the metacarpals on the feet.

Themselves here is the object of the verb *embarrassed*. When we use a reflexive pronoun, we are saying that something did something to itself, which means that a reflexive pronoun will be an object in a sentence:

"We certainly made fools of ourselves," they said.

Warning: As much as the Grammar Gram hates to admit it, quite a few people make up reflexive pronouns; they say *theirself* or *themself* instead of *themselves* and *ourself* instead of *ourselves*. These created words don't make sense because they mix a singular and a plural.

If you want to do something nice for *yourself* today, hit *yourself* in the patella to check your reflexes; then study this Grammar Gram to check your reflexives.

THE MAN WITH TWO BRAINS

A good Steve Martin movie and a problem with singulars and plurals

Sometimes, the Grammar Gram is told, a teacher looks out despairingly at a class and cries,

I just wish you all would use your brain just once today! (no)

And with that sentence, the teacher has delved into the realm of science fiction. The sentence makes it sound as if all the members of the class share a single brain; it must be like one of those composite, universal brains in *StarTrek*. The Grammar Gram can picture Captain Kirk looking out on such a class, all sharing one throbbing, pulsating brain. Yuck. What should the teacher have said? Easy enough:

I just wish you all would use your brains just once today!

Somtimes, then, we run into a little trouble when we try to talk about a group and a characteristic they share. Sometimes it's hard to figure out what to make plural. Let's look at another sentence:

Whoopi Goldberg, Sting, and Young MC have one thing in common: they all use a stage name. (no)

Here it sounds as if they all call themselves by the same name; perhaps they all use *Bob*, for instance. Our first instinct is to make the noun at the end plural:

Whoopi Goldberg, Sting, and Young MC have one thing in common: they all use stage names.

This is actually OK, but there is still a nagging suspicion that this version might mean that each uses several stage names. The best solution for this sentence, then, is to make the ending noun singular:

Whoopi Goldberg, Sting, and Young MC have one thing in common: each uses a stage name.

Another troublesome pattern involves an opening phrase:

Throughout their childhood, most children want to change their names. (no)

Although adding an *s* to *childhood* will do, the cleanest solution would be to drop *their* in the first part. By dropping *their*, we are now referring to the idea of childhood, neither singular nor plural.

Throughout childhood, most children want to change their names.

The variations on troublesome singulars versus plurals are endless:

Throughout their career, the Temptations did well. (refers to their career as a group)
Throughout their careers, the Temptations did well. (refers to individual careers)

Children recite "Sticks and stones . . ." when they have been called a name. (Does this mean a particular name?)

Children recite "Sticks and stones . . ." when they have been called names. (Now does it mean that they have been called more than one name?)

These can make your head spin after a while. When the spinning stops, revert to the prime directive: change the sentence to avoid the problem.

US, THE PEOPLE

Let's not make a federal case out of this.

One day in 1776, crowds were gathered outside Independence Hall in Philadelphia waiting for the signers of the Declaration of Independence to arrive. When one of their favorites, John Hancock, stepped out of his stretch carriage, the crowd went wild, screaming, "It's him! It's him!" And poor grammar thus became a part of American history. They should have yelled, "It's he! It's he!" This Grammar Gram will try to sort out why.

In English, a word sometimes changes form when it changes function; for example, the subject *I* becomes *me* when it is an object, *mine* or *my* when it is possessive. But what's the problem? Usually what follows a verb is an object, as in "Tom Paine whines too much; ignore him." In addition, we think of a subject, *she*, for instance, as coming before a verb: "Barbara Fritchie is a great woman; she saved the flag."

But when we use the verb be, we don't follow it with an object; there's no action, so there can't be an object. Therefore, "It is he" is correct, even though it sounds terrible to many people. Think about how you answer the phone. Are you excruciatingly correct? If so, you say, "This is she" or "This is he." Do you mumble "That's me" or "This is her" under your breath? Or do you cheat, avoiding the problem by replying, "Speaking"? The conflict here is between what for many people is comfortable speech ("It's me") and what is grammatically correct ("It is I"). If this were a problem only in speaking, however, it wouldn't be in this Grammar Gram. It does affect our writing:

Hamilton wrote that. The federalist you should talk to is he.

Yes, this is the correct way to write the sentence. A way to test it is to flip the sentence around: "He is the federalist you should talk to." Since it works in both directions, we have the correct case here. But simply because the sentence is correct doesn't mean that it sounds nice—and it doesn't. We can change it:

Hamilton wrote that. You should talk to him.

The very worst kinds of sentences with case problems are those in which you can't quite sort out what the word should be doing. For instance, which of the following is correct?

Must the enemy we fight always be they? Must the enemy we fight always be them?

Although we can say, "Must we always fight them?" we can also say, "Must they always be the enemy?" Here the only way to decide is to drop the least important words from the sentence and find the core, the basic idea:

Must the enemy be they?

Turn the sentence around to double-check: "Must they be the enemy?" *They*, then, is the correct form. No object involved. But often we can't decide or the sentence sounds terrible. In that case, rely on the prime directive: rewrite the sentence to avoid the problem:

Must they always be the enemy we fight?

When the framers of the Constitution were trying to decide on that first word, they probably turned to *Ye Olde Grammare Gramme* and found that *us* is the object and *we* the subject. Thus the sentence, luckily, turned out to be grammatically correct:

We the people. . . do ordain and establish this constitution for the United States of America.

Note: The Grammar Gram thinks that *him, me, them,* and the other objects are gradually winning. Don't be surprised if, in your lifetime, it will be considered acceptable to use these objects where today the very correct use subjects.

THAT'S ALL VERY *WELL* AND *GOOD*

But what's the difference?

On most days, the Grammar Gram feels *good*: the sun shines and the daily paper contains only one or two grammatical errors. On those days, the Grammar Gram feels *good about life.*

On most days, too, the Grammar Gram feels *well*; that is, the Grammar Gram is healthy, not sick. One distinction between *good* and *well* then, might be that *good* expresses a general sense that all is right with the world while *well* expresses an almost medical opinion about one's health. But don't think that the distinction is always that clear. Look at the following:

I try to do good every day. I am a good person.

Good in the first sentence is a noun that means nearly the same as *good deed.* In the second sentence, *good* is an adjective that makes a value judgment. But now look at another pair:

As a saint, I try to do well in everything I attempt. But I am not a well person.

In the first, *well* is an adverb, telling about the quality or success of the activities. Health (perhaps mental health) is the focus of the second sentence. The following sentence combines both words:

People like Gordon Gecko often do well, but they rarely do good.

We are saying that these people make a great deal of money but don't help people very much. But enough of Wall Street—let's go to the hospital. If the doctor says, "The patient is doing good," we should assume that the patient is walking through the wards, perking up the spirits of everyone in the hospital. And if the doctor says, "The patient is doing well," we can breathe a sigh of relief: the wound caused by the errant discus is healing nicely. Please be aware, however, that in casual conversation to say, "She's doing very good," in reference to health is common and not the worst thing you can say. But do try to avoid it.

There is a very general rule hiding in here: if you're talking about an activity, use the adverb *well*; if you're talking about a state of being (as with *is*), use the adjective *good*:

"Saint Gecko" sounds good but probably won't be well received by the pope.

Here *sounds* does not actually indicate an activity, but *received* clearly does. Read it again and you will see how clear this actually is. But in the meantime, if someone asks you how you are feeling, you can always cheat and say,

I'm feeling fine, thank you.

And of course, to say, "You sure do feel good" may have more than one meaning that we probably don't want to get into right now.

THE SUN ALSO RISES, TOO

When and where to use also, too, *and* in addition

Sometimes phrases just seem to come out right the first time. It's hard to imagine the wicked witch in *The Wizard of Oz* screaming, "And your little dog, in addition!" The woman may have been a witch, but she knew that *too* was the appropriate way to end that sentence. It can be hard, however, to decide between *also, too, in addition*, and *additionally*.

When starting a sentence, choose *in addition* over *also*, and especially over *too*. Don't say, "It snows on Kilimanjaro. Also, it gets very stormy." Although, strictly speaking, this is correct (because *also* acts like *however* or *therefore*), it is awkward. Instead, say,

It snows on Kilimanjaro. <u>In addition</u>, it gets very stormy.

You can use *also* and *too* in this sentence, just not at the beginning:

It snows on Kilimanjaro. It <u>also</u> gets very stormy.
It snows on Kilimanjaro. It gets very stormy, <u>too</u>.

Note: Avoid *additionally* as a substitute for *in addition*.

When connecting two ideas or adding to a list, don't use *also* in place of *and*, because *also* is not a coordinator. Don't say, "The old man caught a big fish, also a bad sunburn." Here you have several choices:

The old man caught a big fish <u>and</u> a bad sunburn.
The old man caught a big fish; he <u>also</u> caught a bad sunburn.
The old man caught a big fish; he caught a bad sunburn, <u>too</u>.

When deciding between *too* and *also*, consider the place in the sentence. A general (not infallible) rule is that *also* should never go at the very end of a sentence, and *too* should never go at the very beginning. Don't say, "His books are concerned with macho activities, and it is clear that he was also." Instead, say,

His books are concerned with macho activities, and it is clear that he was, <u>too</u>.

Also will usually come before the word or words it modifies; *too* can float a little more. In fact, sometimes the meaning can change when *too* moves around:

She, <u>too</u>, found a clean, well-lighted place

implies that someone else also found such a place. But

She found a clean, well-lighted place, <u>too</u>

could mean that someone else also found such a place or that she found a clean, well-lighted place and she also found something else—a book to read, perhaps.

Finally, you should know that the title of this Grammar Gram is the twisted version of the Hemingway novel *The Sun Also Rises*. Also, you should know that he took the title from the Bible. (Are you happy with that last sentence?)

EVO OR DEVO?

Changes in the meanings and uses of words

One of the most popular of the early New Wave rock groups was Devo, which was short for *devolution*, meant to convey the opposite of *evolution*: that is, going backward. Some people who write about English think that every change is for the worse, that our language was once better than it is now. Of course, that's not true.

More often than not, language and writing change by simplifying and collapsing. *Toilet*, for example, used to refer only to the act of washing, grooming, and dressing. Now, of course it only means the porcelain fixture or sometimes the room. But words can take on new meanings, too: *mad* used to mean only "insane"; now it can also mean "angry." While acknowledging that language changes, we should also fight gently to preserve some distinctions. So here the Grammar Gram humbly proposes four pairs of words that it would be nice if we could keep distinct—if only for fun.

eager vs. anxious *Anxious* means "upset or nervous." *Eager* means "enthusiastic, looking forward to something." Oddly, we often use *anxious* when we should probably use *eager*, and we have done so for years. We probably shouldn't say, "I am anxious to leave for Leavenworth," but should say,

> I am eager to leave for Leavenworth, although thinking about Leavenworth makes me anxious.
> I eagerly await my release, as I anxiously await the jury's verdict.

irritate vs. aggravate *Aggravate* means "to make worse," while *irritate* means "to annoy." Hence we shouldn't say, "The long drive to Sing Sing aggravates me," but should say,

> The long drive to Sing Sing irritates me; thinking about it aggravates my depression.
> The judge told me not to aggravate the situation by shouting; his remarks irritated me.

imply vs. infer *Imply* means "to suggest"; it's what the writer does. *Infer* means "to deduce, gather from"; it's what the reader does. We can say, then,

> The birdman implied that Alcatraz was no Club Med.
> The warden seems to be implying that the birdman liked Kentucky Fried Chicken.
> We can infer that he didn't like Alcatraz any better than Devil's Island.

comprise vs. consist of *Comprise* means "to include or contain," whereas *consist of* means "to be made up of." The meanings are similar but not interchangeable; the most common error involves mixing the two verbs and ending up with a sentence such as "The French penal system was comprised of the Bastille and several smaller prisons." We cannot say "comprised of." No. Never. But we can say,

> The compound at Botany Bay comprised several acres.
> The list of prisoners comprises ten volumes.
> The device in "The Penal Colony" consists of tiny glass needles that poke the convict's skin.
> Punishment consisted of writing the convict's sentence on his skin with needles.

Many dictionaries list the forbidden uses above as becoming acceptable. The world won't fall apart if the distinctions between these words disappear, but perhaps we won't have quite as many neat things to say. Then again, some new ways to say things will come along. Or did you already *infer* that?

CAN YOU BE MORE SPECIFIC?

Dear Grammar Gram:

In a memo, I recently wrote, "We can divide the donation into specified amounts." A reviewer of the memo wrote back that it should be "specific amounts," commenting that "*specified* is a verb transient that denotes action." When I asked the reviewer if the verb *specified* was homeless as well as transient, the reviewer didn't laugh. It's hard to have fun with English.

Sign me,
"Joan Rivers"

Dear "Joan" (the GrGr doesn't believe that's your real name),

It isn't hard to have fun with English; it's only hard to have fun with people.

Using verbs as adjectives is a fairly common (and safe) activity:

We heated the pool every day. (verb)
We had a heated argument. (adjective)

I covered the wagon with a tent. (verb)
May I park my covered wagon in the garage? (adjective)

Why, it seems like just yesterday that we anodized the aluminum.
Do you have any spare anodized aluminum? (adjective)

Therefore, there is no difficulty in saying either "We can divide the donation into specified amounts" or "We can divide the donation into specific amounts." But be aware that there is a slight difference between *specific* and *specified. Specified* implies "already determined," whereas *specific* implies "certain" but does not imply that those amounts have been already set. Other verbs, too, carry a meaning slightly different from the adjective's meaning:

Your horse looks mighty pacific.

This means that your horse looks peaceful, calm. But the verb acting as adjective produces a different meaning:

Your horse looks mighty pacified.

Now the sentence means that you have done something to calm the horse down.

The Grammar Gram has checked with a variety of lesser grammar gurus, and none has heard of the phrase "verb transient," although perhaps it was used in a previous era. It sounds rather like a term of heraldry: "The coat of arms for the Grammar Gram family is a verb transient on a sheet of blank paper and a sentence fragment couchant in a paragraph." (You may want to look up *heraldry* and *couchant* in a dictionary.) However, a "transitive verb" is one that has an object: *eat* is one, as in "We just ate dinner."

The final point of this grammar gram is not the conflict between *specific* and *specified.* It is that acceptability cannot always be determined by consulting a dictionary. Some dictionaries list *specified*, for example, only as a verb, while others list it as both a verb and an adjective. Therefore, common sense and common usage should also be your guide.

Sic transitive gloria mundi,
The Grammar Gram

DOUBLE INDEMNITY

Making the reader pay twice for the same idea

Double Indemnity is a wonderful book (by James M. Cain, written in 1936, and made into a movie starring Barbara Stanwyck and Fred MacMurray in 1944). In the law, *double indemnity* means that an insurance company will pay twice the amount of the insurance if a death is accidential. In writing, it means that we are making the reader pay twice because we're repeating ourselves.

Sometimes we repeat ourselves because we try too hard to be correct. We try to please our readers by being precise, and we sometimes overdo it, adding qualifiers to words that either don't need them or shouldn't have them.

1. Sometimes we tack on a preposition, even though we've used it already.

It's the seamy world of insurance fraud in which the book is set in. (no)
It's the seamy world of insurance fraud in which the book is set. (yes)
Is Mr. Nirdlinger the guy from whom you took the crutches from? (no)
Is Mr. Nirdlinger the guy from whom you took the crutches? (yes)

2. Sometimes we qualify a word that can't be qualified.

Lola was wearing a somewhat unique dress. (no)
Lola was wearing a unique dress. (yes)

Unique means "one of a kind"; therefore, saying "somewhat unique" doesn't add anything to the original word. However, we have qualified it so much over the years that the meaning of the word has almost changed from "one of a kind" to "out of the ordinary." But not yet. How would you change the following?

Phyllis asked Walter to keep their discussions about insurance very confidential. (no)
Pricing black dresses before he was dead was somewhat thoughtless of her. (no)

Either it's confidential or it's not; either you think or you don't.

3. Sometimes we say the same thing twice with different words.

The train to Santa Barbara moved slowly, but yet fast enough to kill someone. (no)
The train to Santa Barbara moved slowly, yet fast enough to kill someone. (yes)

Phyllis Nirdlinger's past history should have revealed her mental problems. (no)
Phyllis Nirdlinger's history should have revealed her mental problems. (yes)

4. Sometimes we say it twice because once doesn't seem enough.

Nettie was a faithful and devoted servant. (no)
Nettie was a faithful servant. (yes)

They wanted a casual, informal atmosphere. (no)
They wanted a casual atmosphere. (yes)

5. Sometimes we pile up so much that we lose all sense.

He is Los Angeles's oldest living retired former insurance adjuster. (no!)

Oldest implies that he is still alive, so drop *living. Former* implies retired, so drop either one.

Let us end with a proclamation that combines sins 2 and 5 above: that is, it uses a word that can't be qualified without a complete loss of sense: "That's guy's a virgin—or at least he's very close to being one."

MAY WE CHECK YOUR REFERENCES?

This, that, these, those, they, them, it

That's how we sometimes end a paragraph or begin a sentence, especially when we haven't had enough sleep. If you think there's something missing in the sentence you just read, you're right. *That* doesn't refer to anything. Following are some of the most troublesome areas involving *that* and its pals listed in the subtitle.

BROAD REFERENCE

Look at the following paragraph, paying particular attention to the last sentence.

> "Sunday. Towasaurus Wrex, the meanest monster truck, meets Bigfoot V, the biggest of all the monsters." Radio and television spots like this tell us that monster truck mania is sweeping the country. But what do you do with a monster truck? Can you take it to the drive-in? Should your in-laws buy one? That's what we'll be discussing in this paper.

Just what will we be discussing? We can perhaps figure it out, but the writer is using *that* too broadly. Here, probably the best version of the last sentence is "We'll be discussing these questions . . . " Here's another:

> Monster trucks need names that will be popular with their fans. To achieve this, owners call them such things as Orange Crush, Thumper, Master of Disaster, Big Brutus, Awesome Kong, and Top Dawg.

To achieve what? *This* refers to a vague notion not spelled out in the preceding sentence. The Grammar Gram Major Rule of Reference (GGMRR) should help us here: if we use a pronoun such as *that*, we must be able to replace it with a word or phrase from what we have just said. In our example, we can change the first sentence to "Popularity is the goal in choosing names for monster trucks." Then the *this* in the second one can refer to *popularity*. Let's do one more in which the pronoun *that* can be replaced with a word or phrase:

> Monster trucks don't just crush smaller trucks and slosh through mud at county fairs. Challenging each other in serious races is an important part of their lives. In fact, that's what most monster trucks were built for.

Here we can substitute *challenging each other in serious races*, for *that*, so this reference in fact works.

PREREFERENCE

As you read the next example, notice when you first discover what *that* refers to.

> The Eliminator, the Intimidator, and Grave Digger are all tough-guy names. That's what we look for in a monster truck: a tough-guy image.

Rather than referring to something that came before it, "that" turns out to refer to something that comes later. However, if handled correctly, prereference can create a little suspense: "It's true: your truck is your life."

CONFUSING REFERENCE

Of the three types of reference errors, this is the easiest to spot and the least troublesome:

> Most monsters are Chevys, but one is a Toyota and one is a stretch limousine. It's an amazing thing to see.

We assume that the pronoun "it" refers to the closest preceding noun: *limousine*. But readers will be a little uncertain. If it is truly just the limousine, we might say, "The limo is an amazing thing to see."

That's all you need to remember. (A good reference or not?)

CAN'T WE AGREE ON ANYTHING?

Dear Grammar Gram:

I am in a real pickle. (Well, no, it's not a real pickle, but it is a pickle. No, it's more like a jam.) I am unable to agree with anyone about anything. Every time I start a sentence, I can't reach an agreement.

Signed,
Disagreeable

Dear Dis:

Agreement, of course, means that subjects and verbs, nouns and pronouns must match: if the subject is singular, the verb will be singular; if the verb is plural, we have a plural subject. Most of the time we don't have problems with agreement; we begin a sentence with "The lonely lapidaries" and since the noun is plural, we know that our verb will be plural: "are languishing in Latvia." But here we'll talk about some troublesome sentences.

SOME COMPOUND SUBJECTS CAUSE PROBLEMS.

If your lobster or you (is?) (are?) longing for licorice, try learning some lyrics instead.

The correct word here is, in fact, *are.* In sentences that connect two subjects with *or,* we make the verb agree with the subject closest to it. If we turn the sentence around, we switch the verb:

If you or your lobster is longing for licorice, try learning some lyrics instead.

If the second subject is plural, the verb will be plural, too:

Langston and the Leungs are looking languidly at the lobelia.

With some compound subjects, however, only you as the writer can decide. Are they one unit or separate?

Information and assistance in leasing lemurs is (are) available in the lobby.

"MORE" PROBLEMS.

More than one lepidopterist I know is looking for a new loft or other lodging.

In this sentence, we are clearly talking about "more than one," but we still make it singular. Using *are* here doesn't even sound correct—which is good, because it isn't. But if we had said, "More than a dozen lepidopterists," we would have said, "are looking."

TITLES, WORDS AS WORDS, AND PROPER NAMES ARE SINGULAR, EVEN IF THEY ARE PLURAL.

That's not as weird as it sounds. Look at the following:

The Letters, produced in 1973, is a small movie.
Marbles is a word I enjoy rolling around in my mouth.
The Two Rivers is a small town in northern Saskatchewan.

Grammar Grams are (is?) just one of many resources for learning about agreement.

The Grammar Gram

TAKE *THAT,* AND *THAT,* AND *THAT*

Three times to use that *word*

Often *that* is just an unnecessary word, the vermiform appendix (look it up) of many otherwise wonderful sentences. But sometimes we do need to use it; the writer of the following sentence should have used *that*:

I read in the paper where the fashion police found his gold lamé platform shoes in the river. (no)

Literally, this means that the location where the shoes were found (just south of Battery Park, perhaps) was reported. Although that may be the case, more often than not what the writer means to say is

I read in the paper that the fashion police found his gold lamé platform shoes in the river.

The paper, then, simply reported *the fact that* the shoes were found at all, not *where* they were found. The sentence below is closely related to this first example:

The sergeant told us how they discovered his red polyester shirt, together with a set of gold chains, tucked inside an old Bee Gees album. (no)

Did the sergeant explain to us the process by which they made the discovery? Probably not. More than likely, the correct word here is not *how* but *that*.

The sergeant told us that they discovered his shirt . . .

Neither error is a mortal sin in speaking, because such *wheres* and *hows* rarely confuse us. But written words seem to carry more weight, and we tend to take them at their face value. When someone writes *how*, we expect that the writer means *how*.

Finally, sometimes we use a comma when what we actually need is a *that*:

The most peculiar thing is, the white disco suit was never recovered.

The comma here needs to go. In its place we'll use *that*.

The most peculiar thing is that the disco suit was never recovered. (no)

We need *that* because the most peculiar thing is not the suit itself but *that the suit was never recovered*. But since some of us are conditioned not to overuse *that*, of course the one time we need it, we drop it and use a comma (even though we know very well that just one comma smack dab in the middle of a sentence doesn't mean anything except that we are out of breath and afraid that some kind of punctuation should be there). Note that sentences using forms of *be* are the ones that need *that*. Others, like the following, can get by without *that*, because there's no misunderstanding:

He pretended (that) he was taking karate lessons, but in fact he was learning the hustle.

So the final rule is, if you're tempted to use a comma after the verb, think about using *that* instead. If you read right through the last sentence without correcting it ("final rule is *that* if you're . . . "), then this lesson hasn't sunk in.

THE *TODAY* SHOW

With uninvited guest, the possessive apostrophe

The *Today* show, with hosts from Dave Garroway to Deborah What's-her-name, has had all kinds of guests. And the word *today* sometimes has a guest—an uninvited one, the possessive apostrophe. *Today* in English has two meanings:

1. The specific 24-hour time period we are in right now (you know: not yesterday but today)

2. More generally, the present time: the period or era in which we are living

It's that second meaning, combined with an apostrophe, that gets us into trouble, as in the following: "Today's teenagers face too many choices when it comes to Irish heavy metal folk bands."

We don't actually intend to indicate possession here, as if somehow those teenagers belong to today; all we want to do is explain what time period we are talking about: people who are teenagers today. We might change it to "Teenagers of today face . . . ," but even the *of* is unnecessary (and in fact, the *of* still indicates possession). Why not just say,

Teenagers today face too many choices when it comes to Irish heavy metal folk bands.

But it's not just those teenagers today we need to watch out for; it's also society, as in "In today's society, Norwegian acoustic salsa just hasn't caught on." Again, just say,

In society today, Norwegian acoustic salsa just hasn't caught on.

In most cases, *today's* acts like an adjective meaning "modern" or "contemporary," and either of those words would be just fine: *today's rock musicians* then becomes *modern rock musicians, contemporary rock musicians*, or *rock musicians today.*

Even more dangerous and deadly is a famous triple redundancy we sometimes use to make our point: "In *today's modern, fast-paced society,* people are looking for a little light heavy metal." Ugh. Please, just pick one: *In society today, In modern society, Today.*

But that's not to say that *today* never takes a possessive apostrophe. Sometimes it does when we mean the present 24-hour period—but even here, it's usually considered to be quite casual (and we can usually change it easily): *Today's soup* is fine, but it could just as easily be *the soup today*, and *today's stock market report* is also fine, but so is *the stock market report today.*

Note that *yesterday* and *tomorrow* work the same way that *today* does: avoid, if you can, saying, "Yesterday's cars were better built." Say, "Cars in the past . . . "

Remember that in the universe of grammar and writing, making *today* possessive is not a serious crime. However, the next time you see an advertisement that reads, "Today's Bathroom Fixtures at Yesterday's Prices," take this Grammar Gram to the store owner, and suggest the following wording:

Modern Fixtures at Old-fashioned Prices.

Remember: In today's world, good grammar is everybody's business.

THE PERIODIC TABLE

We're withholding information.

Sentences, as we all know, come in all shapes and sizes, from simple little things like "Please stay away" to bigger ones that would cover this page. (It's true. Look in any novel by William Faulkner.) Most sentences just roll from our pens however they want to, with probably not as much attention from us about their form as there should be. Two wonderful kinds of sentences don't always spring naturally from our minds and pens. Therefore, in this Grammar Gram and the next one, we'll talk about periodic sentences and cumulative sentences, and then you need to go practice them.

Remember that in the simplest kind of sentence, we begin with a subject and then add a verb: that's our main thought. In a *periodic sentence*, we withhold the main idea, or most of it, until the end. Why would we want to do such a thing? First of all, such a sentence can create suspense. (That doesn't mean that our readers will be hiding their eyes in terror, but it does mean that they'll be wondering what's coming next.) In addition, by putting modifying material first, we are making it more important, highlighting it.

Periodic sentences can take an infinite variety of forms. Most often, they are short:

> Hoping for salvation and for release from the kennel, the bulldog bided his time.

In a sentence like this, we get a great deal of information, but until the comma we have no idea who is hoping. It does, however, make us concentrate on the opening phrase. Here are several other, longer forms, with the main points underlined:

> If I had been a smarter dog, if I had waited (as I had intended to do) for the right moment instead of jumping right in with all four feet, I might not be in this pickle.

Such "If . . . then" sentences are some of the most common periodic sentences. Notice that we can often omit *then.* Here's another kind:

> Every spring of my puppyhood, as soon as the snow melted and the first crocuses burst through the warming ground and buds swelled on the apple blossoms that surrounded the kennel, we would pay a visit to the old dachshund who lived in the back of the yard.

Rather than a whole clause as in the first example, here we have just a long modifier, in this case acting as an adverb, because it tells us when the visits took place. Here's one with a slightly different arrangement:

> The common dog one meets on the street, a mangy mutt of indistinct heritage and distinct ribs, scrapping for bones with some equally unkempt mongrel (whose manners are worse than those of the lowest street urchin), may live a mean, shallow life, but is at heart an optimist.

In this case we have begun the sentence with the subject and have then inserted a great deal of material before the verb. All that material does is modify *dog*, explaining more about the dog.

Rule: Punctuation inside periodic sentences must be both extremely accurate and helpful. A long periodic sentence with incorrect punctuation may turn into a heap of words out of which neither you nor the reader can crawl.

If writers knew how fascinating periodic sentences are to write, and if readers knew how fascinated they become when they read periodic sentences, they would study this Grammar Gram very carefully.

SERIOUS AND CUMULATIVE

Are those sentences or clouds?

In Grammar Gram X.1, we talked about periodic sentences, those in which the main idea is delayed until the end. In this Grammar Gram, we will talk about the other end of the spectrum: *cumulative sentences.* In these sentences, we open with the subject and the verb but then add on material, building and building. Often in these sentences the readers' first reaction is different from their final reaction. Just as we can use periodic sentences to build suspense, we can use cumulative sentences to surprise and twist things a little. Look, for instance, at a simple little sentence:

Pluto considers himself a dog.

Nothing to it. It's all very clear and straightforward. Now let's jazz it up:

Pluto considers himself a dog, a *Canis familiaris*, and not some cartoon mutt with anthropomorphic pretensions like Goofy—neither dog nor human but bizarre caricature.

The main idea is the same, but we have something completely different here. And it was fairly easy to produce; we simply (and very carefully) piled modifier on modifier until we reached our point. Like periodic sentences, cumulative sentences are infinite in variety. Let's look at one that's not very complicated:

However, Pluto too must decide what he is: a doberman? a chihuahua? perhaps (God forbid) just a mutt?

The material that we've added to the end of the sentence is not absolutely essential, but it certainly gives some flavor to a shortish sentence. Here's another in a slightly different pattern:

She's a dog's kind of dog, not waiting around all teary and neurotic by the door for the folks to come home from work but out there in the yard at her job, digging, scratching, sniffing, and otherwise performing the activities demanded of her species since dinosaurs passed from this earth.

By now you might be noting that these are easier to write and to read than periodic sentences, perhaps because we get the subject and verb out of the way. We aren't waiting for them. Let's look at one more:

The Beagle Boys sat demurely on their haunches, looking for all the world like cuddly—but terribly ugly—stuffed toys instead of the vicious cartoon crooks they actually are.

Rule for both cumulative and periodic sentences: Like all good things in life, these aren't as much fun if you use them too often. Use 'em; don't abuse 'em.

To get you going on the path to cumulative sentences, the Grammar Gram is donating the following main idea, along with three choices for adding things. It's up to you to finish the sentence. Pick one, or try all three ways:

A big dog like Marmaduke is happiest at home, sitting __________.
A big dog like Marmaduke is happiest at home, secure in __________.
A big dog like Marmaduke is happiest at home, where __________.

By the way, the Grammar Gram did want to mention that the clouds are cirrus (the wispy ones stretched out like thin feathers) and cumulus (the big puffy ones).

ELEVEN FUN THINGS YOU CAN DO IN WRITING

Here are some things to try sometime. Writing is fun when you get to take chances based on your knowledge of the basics and of your audience. These techniques also create a voice, a character in your writing. Be bold. Don't wait for a safe moment. But then, don't blame the Grammar Gram if someone thinks you're wrong or weird. Beware: Not all of these work in every situation, and they work only if used sparingly.

1. Use hyphens to make up a new modifier:

It was one of those it's-just-us-fools-here moments we love to see in Congress.

2. Interrupt a sentence with a question or an exclamation inside parentheses:

When Congress voted for National Yard Equipment Rental Week (did they have nothing better to do?), several younger members showed up in shorts.

3. Use a dash to surprise us at the end of a sentence:

Congress passed all the laws they needed to last year—except the sensible ones.

4. Ask a rhetorical question and then answer it with one word:

Should senators be allowed outside without adult supervision? Rarely.

5. Answer a *why* question with a *because* fragment:

Why do members of Congress seek reelection? Because they have no job skills.

6. Emphasize a point by starting a sentence with a coordinating conjunction:

Backbones may be lacking in Washington. But guts are in even shorter supply.

7. Repeat small words or phrases for emphasis:

The House has a speaker, the House has members, but the House doesn't seem to have a brain.

8. Omit some commas to achieve a sense of urgency:

"Oh, please please please vote for my porkbarrel," whined the whip.

9. Use a cumulative sentence:

Senators consider themselves to be upholders of our precious freedoms, noble defenders of democracy who will, in the words of President Kennedy, "bear any burden, support any friend, defeat any foe," and, incidentally, accept any free trip.

10. Throw in a periodic sentence:

A really excellent filibuster, complete with Bible readings and dictionary recitations and attended by a few custodians sweeping the floors and selected representatives snoring in their seats, can reaffirm one's faith in our democratic system.

11. Make a prereference:

Most members of Congress are just overgrown kids. It's fun: they try to see who can spit the farthest when they should be balancing the budget.

These ideas and suggestions are covered in various Grammar Grams.

THE SKI PUNKS VERSUS THE TEN COMMANDMENTS

Repetition for emphasis

The Ski Punks have a song in which most of the lyrics are as follows:

> My lodge, my chicks, my beer: get lost. My snow, my skis, my slope: get lost.

And the Ninth Commandment says,

> Thou shalt not covet thy neighbor's house, thou shalt not covet thy neighbor's wife, nor his manservant, nor his maidservant, nor his ox, nor his ass, nor anything that is thy neighbor's.

What do these have in common besides the obvious? They share an understanding of the rhetorical value of repetition. Repeating words, when done carefully, can enhance the meaning and the impact of our statements. In both the song and the commandment, the repetition of small words—*my*, *nor*, and *his*—serves to emphasize each of the individual units. Look what happens when we change the Ski Punks' song:

> My snow, skis, and slope: get lost.

Two things happen in this version. First, we see all three as simply parts of one whole, not as individual elements. Second, we lose the overall effect. The revised version is not as strong; it lacks punch. We almost want to add *please* at the end. The best way to get a sense of the difference is to say both versions out loud. Well. Go ahead. Say them out loud—there, do you hear the difference?

Sometimes the repetition of small words can create slight changes in meaning or intention. Look at the following pair of sentences, both of which are correct:

> Please bring some locusts, frogs, and serpents.
> Please bring some locusts, some frogs, and some serpents.

In response to the first sentence, the Grammar Gram would feel quite in line bringing one locust, three frogs, and two serpents but would feel obligated to bring at least two or three of each in response to the second. In the first one, *some* refers to the whole group; in the second, we repeat *some* to indicate the variety we are after.

Finally, sometimes repetition of larger parts of phrases can also be effective:

> That pharaoh has his own pyramid, sphinx, and temple.
> That pharaoh has his own pyramid, he has his own sphinx, and he has his own temple down there at Abu Simbel.

The first version seems as if we're just listing what the pharaoh has, just taking inventory. In the second one, we're building up to a climax and emphasizing the abundance. It's almost as if the speaker were saying, "And if you're surprised that he has a sphinx, just wait until you hear that he has a temple, too."

Two cautions: (1) Like all good things, too much repetition can be too much of a good thing. But if you use it infrequently and well, it will have a terrific impact. (2) When you repeat for emphasis, use consistent and parallel forms. Don't say, "This is my grammar, my style, and a good structure." Instead, say,

> This is my grammar, my style, my structure. Get lost.

THE MEEK SHALL INHERIT THE EARTH

The power of small words

Nothing satisfies like a big, juicy word: *serendipitous*, for instance, or *defenestration.* But often it's the small words that make or break an idea. Those small words—articles, helping verbs, and adjectives, among others—can alter the implications and even the entire meaning of a sentence. Look at the following two versions of a sentence:

We never shipped a crate of kumquats to Cucamonga.
We never did ship the crate of kumquats to Cucamonga.

Both convey the same basic fact: a crate of kumquats did not go to Cucamonga. But in the first sentence, we are all innocence and surprise: "How could you even suppose that we would do such a thing? Why, we don't even know what you're talking about." In the second one, with the verb change to "never did ship" and then the more specific *the*, we are implying that of course we knew about it, but we didn't do it; perhaps we forgot. Say the sentences out loud: you'll hear the difference.

Of course, we can use this knowledge to lie; it may be that in fact we did know we were supposed to ship the crate, but we forgot. If we use the first sentence, we may be able to weasel out of it. But the Grammar Gram is not trying to teach lying and cheating, merely trying to raise small-word consciousness. Let's look at some other small words with big impact:

I didn't try to open the carton of kohlrabi from Kennebunkport.

This is just a statement. Why should I have tried to open the carton? But with a small change, we change the implication:

I didn't really try to open the carton of kohlrabi from Kennebunkport.

In this sentence, perhaps the speaker made a half-hearted attempt, or perhaps the carton was so severely damaged that it wouldn't have made sense to try to open it. Let's try another set of sentences:

Did you try a taste of the kale from Kalamazoo?

I may be implying that you should try it because it's quite good, or I may simply be inquiring. But one small change, and we have a different matter entirely:

Did you even try a taste of the kale from Kalamazoo?

This suggests a whole dialogue that took place before it was spoken. You are 10 years old and at someone's home for dinner. There's some lovely kale at the table. Your mother loves it. You are sure you'll hate it. She says to the host, "Well, everything was certainly delicious," and then turns to you for agreement. When you don't respond as willingly as she would like, she says—under her breath, "Did you even try a taste . . . ," with the emphasis on *try*. She knows you're a typical finicky 10-year-old eater and is getting tired of it.

These are only a very few of the ways in which a small word can make a difference (. . . in which small words can make the difference). You'll notice others as you write.

FORA AND FAUNA, OR HERE'S SYMPOSIA FOR YOU

Plurals of foreign words

In an otherwise respectable professional journal, the Grammar Gram read the following sentence:

> Below is listed information concerning courses, fora, and symposia offered this year. They will take place in classrooms and auditoria throughout the campus.

After reading the sentence twice, the Grammar Gram came to the conclusion that the writer knew two things: first, how to form plurals of words derived from Latin and Greek; and second, how to impress people.

The Grammar Gram wondered why the writer didn't go all the way and say "Coursi, fora, and symposia." (Well, *coursi* isn't actually a word.) *Fora* in particular is so uncommon as to be nearly meaningless in most writing. It would have been better to say "courses, forums, and symposiums" (not to mention "auditoriums").

The Grammar Gram's snideness is not meant to imply that choosing plurals is always easy. But it is meant to call attention to the desire to use foreign words or endings to make our writing sound more intellectual, even at the expense of clarity.

We have no rules to tell us which words form plurals in which way; we must memorize the uses and forms for each word (don't worry; there aren't very many of them). For instance, we use the Latin plurals for these words:

SINGULAR	PLURAL
Radio is a communication medium.	Are the news media biased?
This datum is incorrect. (more commonly, *piece of data*)	Have you verified these data?

The pairs above are perhaps the most misused of the lot. We rarely think of *medium* and *datum* as the singulars and *media* and *data* as plurals; as a result, sometimes we write "Radio is my favorite news media," when it should be "medium." At other times we use either the original forms or standard English plural forms:

matrix	matrices/matrixes	syllabus	syllabi/syllabuses
colloquium	colloquia/colloquiums	index	indicies/indexes

Audience is the key here. Some professional societies, for instance, might use the word *colloquia* as a matter of course, while others would use *colloquiums*. And the Grammar Gram will of course always vote for the less stuffy, the more common, the more easily understood.

Some words actually change slightly in meaning depending on the kind of plural we attach to them. For instance, *foci* has a rather specific scientific meaning as a plural of *focus*: "the points at which waves or lines converge," as in "The various foci on this chart show our weak points." But the other plural form, *focuses*, can often have a more general, less scientific meaning, as in "You can set six different focuses on this camera." The same is true for *appendix*: your doctor might have taken out six *appendixes* today, but later she might have looked in the *appendices* of an article.

We need to remember that foreign plurals come from many languages, not just Latin and Greek. Those cute little chubby angels are *cherubim* (from Hebrew) in the Bible and in hymns, but in art we call them *cherubs*.

If you find these *phenomena* interesting, perhaps you should add foreign plurals to your *agendum* (or would you say *agenda*?) and avoid *crises* in the future.

SIC TRANSIT GLORIA MUNDI

Fun Foreign Frases

Knowing these words won't get you an A or a raise, but they're good to know. Generally, if a word is still considered to be a foreign word, we put it in italics. While some of the words may not be familiar to you, they are considered part of the English language and need not be italicized.

FROM LATIN

a priori Deductively; based on theory rather than experience: "'Your a priori reasoning won't help us now,' cried Howard the Duck."

ad hoc For the particular purpose at hand; not intended for wider application: "Amazon Women from the Moon is an ad hoc group formed to find mates."

ad infinitum Forever; to infinity.

ad nauseam To the point of illness; overdone: "That Terror from Tiny Town talked ad nauseam about his life; I was afraid he would go on ad infinitum."

de facto By fact but not necessarily by right.

de jure By right but perhaps not in fact: "Ishtar may be our de facto ruler, but she is not our de jure ruler."

modus operandi "Way of operating"; way of doing things: "I don't like the modus operandi of those 10,000 maniacs."

non sequitur "It does not follow"; something that is not in logical sequence: "We were discussing warts. Your asking about my friend Zardoz is a non sequitur."

per se "By itself"; by its very nature: "The movie per se isn't bad; it's that creature in the lagoon I don't care for."

FROM FRENCH

déjà vu "Already seen"; the sense that what you are experiencing has happened to you before: "I had a sense of déjà vu while watching Zsa Zsa in *Queen of Outer Space*."

double entendre Double meaning, especially if one meaning is a little daring: "Do you think that the title *The Adventures of Flesh Gordon* is a double entendre?"

fait accompli "Completed act"; something that's already done: "Those little green guys from outer space said that Plan 9 was a fait accompli."

faux pas A social error; something that "people just don't do:" "It was a faux pas for that creature with the atom brain to eat those people."

savoir faire An understanding of how things are done; social grace: "Mothra always seems to handle Godzilla with a great deal of savoir faire."

FROM GERMAN

angst A feeling of anxiety, dread, or depression, often without a cause and often neurotic: "All that angst expressed by those killer tomatoes seems a bit much."

gestalt A whole; a structure not derivable from its parts: "It's the gestalt of *Heaven's Gate*, that seems stupid."

(By the way, *sic transit gloria mundi* means "thus passes the glory of the earth.") Put it in italics.

ABBREV.

Common abbreviations of foreign words

We often use abbreviations without thinking about—sometimes even without knowing—what they mean. For instance, do you remember that *p.m.* stands for *post meridiem*? This Grammar Gram, then, is a gift. Here are some of the most common abbreviations, their meanings, and some notes on their usage all in one place. Now you don't have to look them up.

A.D. *anno domini* (in the year of our lord) Most people don't realize that the standard place to put this phrase is *before* the year, not after. Use capitals and periods: "No, the Hanging Gardens of Babylon were built long before A.D. 900."

B.C. *before Christ* This one goes after the date. Use capitals and periods: "The Pharos, or lighthouse, at Alexandria was designed in 270 B.C."

We rarely use A.D. unless the date is early in the millennium (A.D. 250) and might be confused with something before Christ. However, we almost always include B.C. with a date.

ca. or c. *circa* (around or about) This word is sometimes written out. It is most often used when giving approximate dates. Use small letters and a period: "The Colossus of Rhodes, 120 feet high, was created c. 200 B.C." Please don't combine c. with A.D. to produce confusion, as in "He was born c. A.D. 1610."

cf. *conferre* (compare) People often erroneously think that this means "cross-reference" or "see." Keep in mind that it means "compare." Use small letters and a period: "In 457 B.C., Phidias created the statue of Zeus at Olympia, 40 feet high (cf. Colossus of Rhodes)."

e.g. *exempli gratia* (for example) Small letters and periods: "Some buildings (e.g., the Temple of Diana at Ephesus) are among the Wonders of the Ancient World."

etc. *et cetera* (and so on) Caution: don't say, "and etc." It's redundant.

et al. *et alia* (and others) Most frequently used in footnotes and legal documents to indicate other authors, participants, and so on. Period only after *al.* Often frowned on in the following use because we have no idea who the others might be: "Artemisia et al. are credited with building the Mausoleum at Halicarnassus."

ibid. *ibidem* (in the same place) In footnotes, use for the second successive reference to a work. (Think of *ibid.* as verbal ditto marks.) If another footnote comes between the references, use *op. cit.*

i.e. *id est* (that is); cf. *e.g.* This one means that you'll explain, clarify, or restate in a different way: "The Great Pyramid of Khufu (i.e., Cheops) took twenty years to build."

op. cit. *opus citatum* (the work cited) Used in footnotes after an author's name to indicate that you have already given the complete reference.

RSVP *repondez s'il vous plaît* (please respond) This one doesn't quite fit with the others, but the Grammar Gram must point out that the greatest sin in the known universe (next to the Yugo) is to say, "Please RSVP." It shows that you don't know what *RSVP* means. Use capital letters and no periods.

Although we use some of these abbreviations (e.g., A.D. and B.C.) almost exclusively in their abbreviated form, others (esp., *e.g.* and *i.e.*) are frowned on in semiformal and formal writing or restricted to use in parentheses. Know your audience, and when necessary, use the English equiv.

IT'S NOT EASY BEING GREEN

Dear Grammar Gram:

Do you mind if I ask you a question? What's the difference between *Black* and *African-American*? Do we capitalize *white* if we capitalize *Chicano*? What are the rules? Isn't this frustrating?

Signed,
Kermit (None of the above) the Frog

Dear Kermit:

Frustration is a human emotion; the Grammar Gram does not find this frustrating—merely sticky.

WHY DO PEOPLE KEEP CHANGING THE WAY WE REFER TO ETHNIC GROUPS?

Words reflect political and social attitudes, which do change. In addition, some words acquire negative connotations, for which we need to find more neutral replacements. For instance, *Oriental* is no longer acceptable in many places; the negative images attached to it are too strong. Such changes are not limited to ethnic and racial groups: notice the changes from *crippled* to *handicapped* to *disabled*. Each change seeks to give a more positive view of people. Group names probably always will change.

WHAT DO PEOPLE WANT?

The question points out two great dangers. First, it assumes that everyone in a particular group is of a single mind about the group's name. That simply isn't true. Second, we shouldn't ask one member of a group, "What do you people want to be called?" as if green skin makes you speaker for all green-skinned people.

WHAT ARE THE RULES?

There are no rules, only conventions. Sometimes we want the broadest possible categories (*Asian American*), and other times we want a great deal of detail (*Korean American*, *Chinese American*, and so on). One current trend is to use geographic classifications, so we have, for example, *African Americans*, *Asian Americans*, *Mexican Americans*, *Native Americans* and *European Americans*. The Grammar Gram likes these as broad categories; they're parallel and descriptive. They will not, however, satisfy everyone, and they exclude many smaller groups.

POINTS TO REMEMBER

1. Learn and follow current practice, and know that it varies from place to place. Don't get huffy. Don't say, "Well, I'm not going to say 'African American'; I just learned 'Afro-American.' " Don't cling to old forms. Often we don't like a term simply because we aren't used to it. Give yourself time.

2. Be consistent. Try not to mix color (*Black*), geography (*Asian American*), and race (*Caucasian*).

3. If you capitalize one, capitalize them all: not *Blacks* and *whites*, but *Blacks* and *Whites*.

4. Note that many people don't want hyphens (e.g., *Cuban-American*) because the hyphen gives the sense of not being "true" or "full" Americans, that is, "American with a qualification."

5. Remember that these words are deeply involved with emotion, identity, and respect.

The Grammar Gram

GRAMMAR AND THE SINGLE COMMA

Dear Grammar Gram:

I was recently given a comma as a birthday present, and I'm not sure how to use it. I'm very good with pairs of commas, but just one? You know what they say—"Use it or lose it!"—and of course I do want to be careful.

I am,
Curious (Yellow)

Dear C. (Yellow):

The Grammar Gram is glad very glad you asked. Although commas often come in manageable pairs, it's those single ones that get crazy sometimes. Let's start with where *not* to put your comma.

First, never use a single comma between a subject and its verb, as the following does: "*Fanny Hill,* refers to a woman rather than to an oddly shaped mountain." That comma isn't good, no matter how desperate you are to use it. We often drop in such a lonely comma, especially after titles, because we get nervous: we think that perhaps there should be a little something more to go along with that title. *Don't get nervous*: no punctuation should separate a title that is followed by its verb.

Sometimes if a great deal of material comes before the verb, we think we need a comma to tell the reader to take a breath: "The handsome Tom Jones's only obvious connection to the attractive Fanny Hill, is that they are both slightly on the wild side." No comma is needed or wanted. The comma is just a security blanket, an excuse to gasp in big gulps of air because we're afraid the sentence has gone on too long.

Second, don't use a single comma after *but, so, although,* and similar words: don't say, "John Thomas has a small role in some book but, I can't remember which one." The single comma goes before the word:

John Thomas has a small role in some book, but I can't remember which one.

Finally, don't use a comma at the beginning of a line when you run out of space at the end of the previous line:

Sometimes I wonder why people feel so strongly about some books
, *Ulysses*, for instance, that they want to ban them.

Don't laugh. There is nothing weirder in this world (except Buster Poindexter's hair) than that comma hanging there. A comma indicates a pause; but how do we pause when we haven't even gotten going yet?

Well, then, what can you use your single comma for? Use it to separate two independent clauses:

Tropic of Cancer is a good book, but the cartoon version was terrible.

Use it at the beginning or the end of a sentence to set off added comments or clarifications from the main subject and verb:

At first glance, *Lady Chatterley's Lover* is just a stimulating novel. It's more than that, however.

Use it after a dependent clause that begins a sentence:

Although *Last Tango in Paris* was wonderful, I didn't understand it at all.

And, of course, use a single comma after the closing in a letter:

Your servant,
The Grammar Gram

COMMA, COMMA, DOWN, DOOBIE, DO, DOWN, DOWN

The first degree of parenthetical ideas

Neil Sedaka was the first person to use the word *comma* in a rock song. The title of this Grammar Gram is from "Breaking Up Is Hard to Do" (1962). In these Grammar Grams, we will be talking about the three ways in which we can set off material that is not essential, material that we usually call "parenthetical."

If we surround something by commas, we can usually drop it out of a sentence:

Apple maggots, as you know, don't make easy pets.

Here we're just inserting a small reminder to the audience; the basic meaning of the sentence is the same with or without it. The material can be a phrase, like the above, or a single word like that below, and it can go anywhere that is appropriate in a sentence:

Connie Stevens is not related, fortunately, to Mormon crickets or Jiminy Cricket.
Fortunately, Connie Stevens is not related to Mormon crickets or Jiminy Cricket.
Connie Stevens is not related to Mormon crickets or Jiminy Cricket, fortunately.

Rule: If we insert something in the middle, we should surround it with a pair of commas; if we put it at the beginning, a comma follows it; if we put it at the end, a comma comes before it.

Sometimes pairs of commas can change the meaning of a sentence:

His aunt, who works with woolly worms at Woolworth's in Fort Worth, belongs to the Wool Growers.

Here the commas surround material not essential to the sentence. Such material can be dropped out of the sentence without harming its basic meaning: he has an aunt who is a member of the Wool Growers' Association. That she works at Woolworth's is just added, nonessential information. If the other material had been necessary, it would mean that he has more than one aunt. And then we wouldn't have used the commas:

His aunt who works with wooly worms at Woolworth's in Fort Worth is a member of the Wool Growers' Association. But his aunt who specializes in silverfish in Silverton belongs to the National Flyfishing Association.

Read these two examples out loud. The differences are clearer when you can hear the pauses. Commas are such dinky little things, though, that we don't stop to realize that they can do so much. Here's another, shorter phrase that also can change the meaning of a sentence:

Your potato bug, Augratin, is not looking well today.

Here the name of the potato bug is just added information. This use is called an *appositive*; it simply means that we are renaming the noun. The commas here imply that there is only one potato bug: we could just as easily have said, "Your potato bug is not looking well today." But if there were more than one potato bug, we would scrap the commas:

Your potato bug Augratin is not looking well today, but Hashbrown is looking fine.

Not using commas means that we need the name; here we must differentiate between two potato bugs.

Let's end this Grammar Gram with a pair of sentences. You decide what each one means.

The entomologists, say the etymologists, have a rather bug-eyed look.
The entomologists say the etymologists have a rather bug-eyed look.

AND DEATH, I THINK, IS NO PARENTHESIS

The second degree of parenthetical ideas

Our title, from a poem by e. e. cummings, probably means that death is not just a little interruption, after which life goes on. Parentheses do indicate just a little interruption. (Death is more like the period at the end of a sentence.) Although the use and misuse of parentheses is not a life-and-death matter, these are a useful pair of marks. They are the middle-of-the-road way to insert parenthetical ideas; that is, they are slightly stronger than commas and slightly weaker than dashes. Use them in four ways.

1. Use parentheses to add a little information that doesn't need to be too prominent in your sentence.

The chuckwalla population of Chula Vista (California) has nearly doubled this year.

We usually add such information purely for clarification; probably very few people outside California know where Chula Vista is. But how do we know when to clarify and when we're going overboard? In different situations, each of the following might be correct:

We found an encampment of camelopards in Chicago.
The number of asps recently asphyxiated in Athens is astounding.
Axolotl assaults have risen in Athens (Georgia) this year.

Common sense is the only guide here: a city like Chicago probably doesn't need to be followed by the state name, but there are at least two cities named Athens. Normally, we won't need to insert *Greece* because that's what the reader will assume. Only if we are afraid that the reader will be confused do we need to refer to Greece. We would more often refer to Georgia (unless we live in Georgia), because not everyone knows that Athens is also a city in Georgia.

2. Use parentheses to add your own opinion.

Coral snakes remain rare to nonexistent in Coral Gables (thank goodness).

Nothing tricky here. We could have used commas, but parentheses make it more interesting and obvious that it's an aside.

3. Use parentheses to combine information and opinion.

The gecko population of Gila Bend has tripled (to an incredible two per acre).

We're giving the figure but loading the information with the word *incredible*.

4. Use parentheses to insert an entire sentence.

Rattlers in Roanoke (this is a new phenomenon!) reached record highs recently.

Notes: Do not capitalize a sentence inside parentheses; give it end punctuation only if it is an exclamation or a question. Drop the period. (There is one exception: if a sentence in parentheses—like this one—occurs between two sentences, punctuate as you would any sentence.) Parentheses in a sentence do not take the place of other punctuation, as you can see in the following:

Although newts are new in Newton (Mass.), they are not a nuisance.

As you progress through your writing career (an exciting one, we hope) consider the beauties of parentheses (but don't use too many)(especially in the same sentence).

THE 100-YARD DASH: PUNCTUATION FOR THE LAZY?

Give 'em the third degree of parenthetical ideas.

The dash is a perfectly good and proper piece of punctuation (but you'd never know it the way people abuse it). We use it when we want a greater than usual break in a sentence:

It's hard to find high-heeled sneakers—not to mention blue suede shoes—in my size, 13½ DDD.

We could have put the phrase "not to mention blue suede shoes" in parentheses, but it would have seemed like a quiet afterthought or something said out of the corner of the mouth. Or we could have used a pair of commas, but then the phrase would not have stuck out. The dashes here give the phrase emphasis; they make the phrase slightly more astounding, which then reinforces the tone created by the words *not to mention.* We want the phrase to stand out. Think of dashes, then, as loud parentheses.

Sometimes a whole sentence can go between dashes:

That rather large dog in the gold-flecked stiletto heels—he's a rottweiler, I think—is unclear about what the word *heel* means.

In a sentence like this one, we see that something inside dashes, as with parentheses and most pairs of commas, may be left out of a sentence, but those same dashes give whatever is inside them an important role in the sentence. Dashes can come near the beginning or the end of a sentence, too:

Pat Boone was famous for his white bucks—and his singing.
"He's wearin' tan shoes and pink shoelaces"—thus begins the chorus of Dodie Stevens' greatest hit single.

If you read these out loud, you will notice that in all of these, the dashes make us pause and give an extra emphasis to the set-off material.

However, like any other kind of punctuation (except periods at the ends of sentences, of course), dashes must be used sparingly. Do not use them because you're too lazy (or in too much of a hurry) to bother to think of a more appropriate and helpful piece of punctuation. Look at the following:

I can't even distinguish—unfortunately—between espadrilles, espaliers, and quadrilles—some are shoes—I think—and some aren't. Do you wear espadrilles on your shoulders—or is that epaulets—or epithets?

Reading that sentence is like riding in a car with someone who is just learning how to handle a clutch: the sudden stops and starts are liable to give you whiplash. Other punctuation would be better:

I can't even distinguish, unfortunately, between espadrilles, espaliers, and quadrilles: some are shoes (I think) and some aren't. . . .

The punctuation has now been carefully chosen to convey certain things: the colon here indicates an explanation to follow, and the parentheses indicate more insecurity than commas would have.

Don't fall victim to the 100-yard dash—the punctuation for the 1990s—something for writers in a hurry; use it with caution, and it will work for you.

WHAT'S ALL THAT BRACKET ABOUT?

You're [sic], [sic], [sic].

This is going to be easy. There are clear rules and unambiguous uses for brackets. But perhaps we need to explain what brackets are: they are square parentheses; that's not a bad explanation because we use them in ways similar to parentheses. Let's take care of the two least common uses, at least for our purposes. First, brackets play a large role in footnotes and citations; check any large handbook for details. Second, we can use brackets to explain how to pronounce a word, as in the following sentence: "Of all the great rivers, the Yangtze [yang-see] is my favorite." While these are important to know, the following uses are the ones most writers deal with. Notice that almost all of the following uses occur in quotations.

Most commonly, we use brackets around the word *sic*, which in Latin roughly means "thus." We use *sic* inside brackets to cover our rear ends. That is, sometimes we are quoting something that we know is spelled wrong or is grammatically incorrect. We follow the questionable item with [*sic*] to indicate that we know it's questionable, but since it's a quotation, we can't correct it:

> The vice president wrote, "My favorites are the Missississippi [*sic*] and the Monongahela."

Here the writer is indicating to the reader that it was the vice president who misspelled the name. Here's another, in which we indicate that the grammar error is part of the quotation:

> "The Utukok, the Euphrates, and the Utla is [*sic*] on different continents," he claimed.

We also use brackets to clarify aspects of a quotation that would otherwise be confusing to the reader:

> He went on to say, "Of my favorites, it [the Wkra] is the wackiest one."

We use brackets in a sentence like this one because we can't just substitute *Wkra* for *it*; we are not allowed to change quotations. As in the sentence above, we can follow the vague word with the brackets, or as in the version below, we can substitute the bracketed term for the vague term:

> He amused us when he said, "I'm certain that [River Phoenix] is in the Southwest."

Here we have simply substituted *River Phoenix* for *it* (although, of course, the pronoun should be *he* instead of *it*, since River Phoenix is an actor, not a river). And we use brackets to provide information within quotations that we think is necessary:

> "The Zorn [in France] is the last river listed in the atlas," he said proudly.

Using brackets here allows us to provide information on the spot. If we weren't able to do it this way, we would probably have to devote an entire sentence after the quotation explaining where the Zorn is.

Finally, we can use brackets instead of parentheses within parentheses. This is the one use not involving quotations:

> Three rivers (the Madison and the Jefferson [named after the presidents] and the Gallatin) meet at the town of Three Forks, Montana, to form the Missouri.

However, consider possible rewrites before you make too many boxes within boxes.

By now, so hopes the Grammar Gram, you know that in the subtitle, [*sic*], [*sic*], [*sic*] doesn't mean anything. And let us remember the words of the vice president: "[Hawaii] is an island that is right here." But never use brackets to make fun of people by highlighting their mistakes.

HYPHEN-NATION

Dear Grammar Gram:

I have recently been appointed to a sub-committee of the committee on committees; none of us is anti-intellectual, but perhaps we are over-eager. Is our grammar top-notch? Are we over-using hyphens?

Signed,
Sam Gross-Davis

Dear Mr. G-D:

Let's talk about hyphens for prefixes and for two-word modifiers. Hyphenated words usually lose their hyphens as they become more common, which means that it's not always clear whether or not a word should be hyphenated; for example, *co-operative* is now ordinarily written *cooperative*. Here are some rules:

Always hyphenate *self-*, *ex-*, and *all-*:

The all-powerful Subcommittee on Subcommittees
The self-absorbed Chair is now an ex-committee member, a witless wanderer

Notice that *selfabsorbed* looks quite silly without a hyphen; in fact, degree of silliness may be a good rule of thumb for deciding when to use a hyphen.

Always hyphenate a prefix before a proper name:

pre-Columbian; anti-Newtonian; post-Darwinian; ex-Lutheran

The reason for this one should be clear: a capital doesn't occur in the middle of a word.

Always hyphenate when you need to clarify meaning:

She's a monster-truck driver. (She drives big trucks.)
She's a monster truck driver. (She's hell on wheels.)

Usually hyphenate a two-word modifier that comes before the word it modifies:

A well-groomed committee chair is always an asset, but an over-cooked piece of pork is not.

Here the two modifiers act as one. It is not a *groomed* committee chair but a *well-groomed* one.

Don't hyphenate if the modifier comes after the word it modifies:

The chair is not well groomed, but neither is she short tempered.

Again, it should be clear why: in this case, *well* is modifying groomed, and they are not acting as a single word.

Notes: Most words with prefixes (e.g., *non*) or suffixes (e.g., *like*) are not hypenated, but written as one word: *underrepresented* is a good example. Use a hyphen only if you'll end up with a double *i* (*anti-inflammatory*) or the famous triple *l* (*krill-like*)

Final rule: Always check the dictionary to see if a word should be hyphenated. If you're still unsure, hyphenate as little as possible.

P.S. The sequels to "Hyphen-Nation"—"Alien Nation" and "Rhythm Nation"—don't have hyphens.

The Grammar Gram

SPACING: THE FINAL FRONTIER

Rules for confronting space

You've got to be kidding, you're saying (the Grammar Gram can tell, you know), an entire Grammar Gram on spaces? On nothing? On blank spots? Yes. Getting all the spaces done properly in a piece of writing doesn't mean much; it doesn't make you a better person. But it is important, because people expect it to be done right.

GENERAL RULES

1. Use two spaces at the end of a sentence before the next sentence:

   Meet George Jetson. Here's Mr. Cosmo Spacely with George's boy, Elroy.

2. Use one space between a comma, a colon, or a semicolon and the next word:

   They explained their continuing mission: to explore strange new worlds.

3. Use one space on each side of each dot if an ellipsis is in the middle of a sentence:

   His mother said, "That Tom Corbett may be . . . a real space cadet."

4. Use a period followed by evenly spaced dots if the ellipsis is at the end of a sentence:

   She continued, "I wish he wouldn't hang around that Flash Gordon. . . ."

   (It would seem illogical to put the period first, but that's the way it's done.)

5. Don't put a space on either side of a hyphen:

   The Adventures of Buck Rogers in the Twenty-fifth Century

6. Don't put a space on either side of a dash. (To create a dash, use two unspaced hyphens.)

   Captain Midnight—sponsored by Ovaltine—changed his name to Jet Jackson.

7. Don't put a space on either side of a slash when used to present alternatives:

   In specially marked jars of Ovaltine was a decoder ring and/or a membership card.

8. Use one space on each side of a slash when indicating lines of poetry:

   "It's about time; it's about space / It's about people in a very strange place."

9. When typing quotations over three lines long, indent five spaces from both margins and then single-space.

LETTERS AND MEMOS (FROM THE TOP DOWN)

1. Leave four lines between the date and the inside address (that is, whom you are writing to).
2. Leave two lines between the inside address and the salutation.
3. Leave two lines (some people prefer just one) between the salutation and the first paragraph.
4. Leave two lines between the last word and the closing.
5. Leave four lines between the closing and your typed name (room for a flourishing signature).
6. Leave two lines between your typed name and any additional notations such as *cc* or *Encl.*

This Grammar Gram has truly raised nit-   picking to new heights   . Is that spacing correct?

A HUNTING WE WILL GO

Impractical language information: terms of venery

Venery refers to hunting, and in the old days (you know, way back when), terms of venery were names given to groups of animals that were hunted. Some terms have fallen by the wayside, but others are with us today:

A pack of dogs
A pack of wolves
A covey of quail
A flock of geese on the ground,
  a gaggle of geese on the water,
    a skein of geese in flight

We have a hutch of hares, a school of fish, a pod of whales, a cete of badgers, and an exaltation of larks. (In fact, there's a wonderful book of these terms called *An Exaltation of Larks.*) Here are some others: a troop of monkeys, a pride of lions, a swarm of bees (does that mean we have a slime of slugs?).

The Grammar Gram modestly proposes that we develop a list of official group terms that can be applied to family members, business associates, and school and college life. (You know, like "Watch out! Here comes a covey of clerks.") Note: In the previous sentence, the verb is singular, because it refers to the term of venery, which is singular. The following are offered up humbly as suggestions and are not meant to be reflective of anything except a twisted mind. You'll notice that there is space for you to create your own:

FAMILY

A bother of brothers
A snicker of sisters
A worry of fathers
A curfew of mothers

A ________ of aunts
A ________ of cousins
A ________ of sons
A ________________

BUSINESS

An embarrassment of executives
A byte of programmers
A tally of tellers
A ledger of accountants
A vanity of vice presidents

A ________ of receptionists
A ________ of cab drivers
A ________ of presidents
A ________ of janitors
A ________________

COLLEGE AND SCHOOL

A dinette of department chairs
A slouch of students
A denial of deans
A stack of librarians
A pride of provosts at their desks;
  a prance of provosts in a meeting
A preach of professors, but a futility of faculty

A ________ of jocks
A ________ of nerds
A ________________

(And of course you would say "a helpfulness of Grammar Grams," wouldn't you?)

THE BERKELEY TEST OF BASIC GRAMMATICAL AND RELIGIOUS CONCEPTS

A. Match the items in the column on the left with the correct categories in the column on the right.

When I think about . . .	I approach the subject with . . .
1. seeing a misused semicolon	a. disgust
2. someone with twelve items in the nine-item checkout lane	b. abject horror and rage
3. acid rain	c. mild distress
4. a major grammatical error in a memo or published report	d. smugness, bemused detachment, and a feeling of "there but for the grace of God go I"—along with a strong desire gently to correct the offender

B. Fill in the blank with the appropriate answer:

1. I feel ________ about the untimely demise of your nutria.
   a. badly
   b. just awful
   c. bad
   d. slightly nauseated
2. I burned my fingertips recently. As a result, I feel
   a. downright poorly.
   b. badly, because I've lost my sense of touch.
   c. that I should call Jacoby and Meyers for a free consultation.
   d. a conflict between free will and predestination.
3. Which of the following was the sequel to Pat Boone's best selling book *Twixt Twelve and Twenty*?
   a. Between You, Me, and the Gatepost
   b. *Between You and I*
   c. *Between You, Your Mom and Dad, and I*
   d. *Between a Rock and a Hard Place*

C. Match the items in in the column on the left with the correct categories in the column on the right.

1. Sentence fragments	a. innately evil
2. Starting a sentence with *and* or *but*	b. impossible to do in good conscience
3. A split infinitive	c. a sure sign of moral lassitude
4. Ending a sentence with a preposition, as Winston Churchill did in Parliament	d. well, he's dead; maybe now we know why

Where are the answers? Scattered throughout the Grammar Grams, of course.

MANNERS IN LANGUAGE

Thank you for not expressing your true feelings.

While engaging in light party conversation recently, the Grammar Gram was confronted with the following statement: "I can't stand it when people always say 'fine' when you ask them how they are. It's so phony. I certainly never say 'fine' if I'm not."

What we have here is a failure to communicate. Language (and now the Grammar Gram is stealing from two grammarians—Thomas Pyles and John Algeo) serves a variety of functions. For instance, it can be informative—facts, statistics, reports on feelings, and so on; it can be interrogative—a question for which we expect a response; it can be directive—"Get me a martini, quick!"; it can be evocative—certain emotions stirred up in our readers or listeners.

A common function of language with an uncommon name is *phatic language*: speech used to establish an atmosphere of sociability rather than to communicate ideas. This is the kind of language we all engage in, not only in speaking but also in writing, every day—the kind the Grammar Gram was engaging in at the party. Phatic language doesn't mean anything in a literal sense, but it is very important. It breaks ice, indicates friendliness, and keeps us from sitting quietly in corners by ourselves or resorting to animallike grunts when confronted with strangers.

When you walk down the street and see a friend, you say, "How are you?" You are asking this phatically; it is just another version of *hello* when *hello* doesn't seem to be enough. You are not asking it interrogatively; you neither expect nor want a response other than "Fine. How are you?"

However, we all know people who insist on taking us literally. Instead of hearing a phatic question, they hear an interrogative one and insist on providing an informative response: "Well, I'm not really too good today. I didn't sleep well and my gerbil croaked." We are in turn forced to continue the conversation, perhaps resentfully, and come up with another phatic line such as "I'm sorry to hear that." The person has, and the Grammar Gram hates to say it, willfully misunderstood the function of language we are using and has put us in an awkward position—and phatic language is often the only escape from such a position. Even in our dealings with our closest friends and relatives, phatic language helps smooth the path.

Let the Grammar Gram draw an analogy from the world of manners. If you are so clumsy as to spill your mock turtle soup on your host's heirloom tablecloth, you say, "I'm terribly sorry," and your host replies, "It's really nothing. That old tablecloth needed a good cleaning," all the while cursing you in his heart and perhaps getting ready to cry himself to sleep later that night. The host has understood the role that phatic language plays in our lives. The words he spoke were empty of real meaning—indeed, contrary to his real feelings—but they were full of reassurance for you, the clumsy oaf. They also allowed the dinner to proceed to the main course in a comfortable, friendly way.

Phatic language is not dishonest, nor is it phony; it is a way of getting along in the world. To feel obligated to reveal our feelings at every point seems more selfish than healthful.

Although you didn't ask, the Grammar Gram wants you to know that it has been a very rough day. The alarm went off too early; then there were those terrible fragments in the newspaper, followed by a misspelled word in a letter. But how are you?

THE ROOT'S THE SAME

An etymology game

You love *Jeopardy*—right? And *Wheel of Fortune*, too—right? You're smarter than most of the people you work with—right again? Has the Grammar Gram got a game for you, a game that will not only satisfy your competitive spirit but also teach you about the marvels and mysteries of our language kingdom.

Below, the Grammar Gram provides two or three definitions; you provide two words that share a common root. You don't need to derive the root (but you should be able to). The key here, of course, is that the words at first seem to have nothing in common, but their common root shows us the words in a new way. OK, let's try an easy one together:

DEFINITION	WORD	ROOT
A. to embarrass or humiliate	mortify	mort (death)
B. funeral director	mortician	

Easy as pie, right? Well, you're on your own.

	WORD	ROOT
1. A. extremely conspicuous	______	______
B. large disastrous fire	______	______
2. A. inflammation in a joint	______	______
B. to repay	______	______
3. A device to keep rain or sun away	______	______
B. a color from crayon boxes	______	______
C. displeasure or resentment	______	______
4. A. one kind of tooth	______	______
B. short, brief	______	______
C. surgical procedure	______	______
5. A. fallen into ruin, rundown through neglect	______	______
B. semiprecious stone	______	______
6. A. unappealing, revolting	______	______
B. vitality, vigor	______	______
7. A. to look up to	______	______
B. wonderful, supernatural	______	______

Try to find some others yourself. In the meantime, the answers are below.

1. A. flagrant, B. conflagration, Root: flagrare (to burn);

2. A. bursitis, B. reimburse, Root: bursa (purse)—the bursa is a little purselike sac that keeps the bones in a joint from rubbing against each other;

3. A. umbrella, B. burnt umber, C. umbrage Root: umbra (shade);

4. A. incisor, B. concise, C. incision, Root: incidere (to cut);

5. A. dilapidated, B. lapis lazuli, Root: lapis (stone)—"dilapidated" used to refer only to stone buildings when the stones had fallen down;

6. A. disgusting, B. gusto, Root: gustus (to taste);

7. A. admire, B. miraculous, Root: mirari (to wonder at).